The History of Educational Administration Viewed through Its Textbooks

Thomas Glass

with Robert Mason, William Eaton,
James C. Parker, and Fred Carver

SCARECROWEDUCATION

Lanham, Maryland • Toronto • Oxford
2004

Published in the United States of America
by ScarecrowEducation
An imprint of The Rowman & Littlefield Publishing Group, Inc.
4501 Forbes Boulevard, Suite 200, Lanham, Maryland 20706
www.scarecroweducation.com

PO Box 317
Oxford
OX2 9RU, UK

British Library Cataloguing in Publication Information Available

Library of Congress Cataloging-in-Publication Data

The history of educational administration viewed through its textbooks /
   Thomas Glass with Robert Mason . . . [et al.].
      p.   cm.
   Includes bibliographical references and index.
   ISBN 1-57886-080-6 (pbk. : alk. paper)
   1. School management and organization—United States—History.
2. Textbooks—United States—History.   3. School administrators—Training
of—United States—History.   I. Title.
LB2806 .G54   2004
371.2'00973'09—dc22   2003018116

∞ ™ The paper used in this publication meets the minimum requirements of
American National Standard for Information Sciences—Permanence of
Paper for Printed Library Materials, ANSI/NISO Z39.48-1992.
Manufactured in the United States of America.

Contents

Preface   v

1   Introduction: A New Profession and a New Textbook
Literature   1
Thomas Glass

2   From Idea to Ideology: School-Administration Texts,
1820–1914   13
Robert Mason

3   From Ideology to Conventional Wisdom: School-
Administration Texts, 1915–1933   31
William Eaton

4   From Conventional Wisdom to Concept: School-
Administration Texts, 1934–1945   45
James C. Parker

5   A Return to Rhetoric: School-Administration Texts,
1946–1955   75
Fred D. Carver

6   Factualism to Theory, Art to Science: School-Administration
Texts, 1955–1985   87
Thomas E. Glass

7 A Retreat from Theory in an Era of Reform: 1985–2000   109
Thomas E. Glass

8 An Overview: School-Administration Texts, 1820–2000   127
Thomas E. Glass

References   143

Index   153

About the Authors   161

Preface

The idea for this book originated in 1978 among faculty in the Department of Educational Administration at Southern Illinois University at Carbondale. Professor William Eaton contended that four identifiable eras of educational-administration textbooks existed prior to the theory movement affecting the field in the 1950s. Colleagues James Parker, Robert Mason, and Fred Carver agreed and began to search the textbook literature representing each of the four historical eras. From this effort a paper presentation proposal was forwarded and accepted by Division A of the American Education Research Association. The four papers focusing on the four eras of general textbook literature in educational administration were presented in Toronto on April 15, 1978.

The titles of the four identified textbook era papers were (1) Ideal to Ideology: School-Administration Texts from 1820 to 1914, (2) Ideology to Conventional Wisdom: School-Administration Texts from 1915 to 1933, (3) Conventional Wisdom to Concept: School-Administration Texts from 1934 to 1945, and (4) Return to Rhetoric: School-Administration Texts from 1946 to 1955. I heard the four papers in Toronto and was fascinated, as information on textbook literature in educational administration is scarce. The most common discussion occurs in initial chapters of general educational-administration texts. This is usually done in a critical manner as the author explains why previous authors and their viewpoints of administration are in error. I can find no other attempts to both review and analyze the trends of this academic literature, presumably providing an information base for the practice of educational administration.

The four papers rested in a file cabinet for a number of years until a chance communication I had with Fred Carver resulted in a later discussion about the possibility of adding a fifth paper describing the era of the behavioral science–based theory movement. This fifth paper would then complete a chronology and hopefully a published monograph. Also, subsequent conversations with other colleagues suggested that an introduction and overall summary might strengthen the proposed monograph. In 1984 I presented a "fifth" AERA paper that included an overall summary of the previous four papers. In 1986 the five papers and summary were published by Interstate Press and remained in print until the early 1990s.

Since the book's original publication in 1986, the field of educational administration has undergone significant changes. The twenty-first century finds the practice of school leadership and administration to be squarely under the gun of political accountability. National studies find the field to be in disarray, especially higher-education programs preparing future administrators. This state of disorganization is perhaps illustrated by the fact that only one entirely new general-type textbook in the field has been published since 1993. Many general texts originally written in the 1980s now are in their fifth, sixth, or even seventh editions.

The educational-administration textbook literature is now splintered into narrow specialties of finance, law, personnel, leadership, principalship, policy, instructional leadership, planning, assessment, and organization theory. These areas often possess competing theory bases, resulting in widely divergent recommendations or prescriptions for practice. Just as the textbook literature is currently fragmented, so is the field of practice.

This new and updated edition reviews both the change in textbooks and the theory used in educational administration between 1985 and 2000. Especially noted is the current return to the era of conventional wisdom and compendiums of best practice. The book provides readers with a historical view of both the field and the textbooks shaping its practice. The two seem to be dependent on each other for content and continuity. What seems to be much needed today is a unifying group of textbooks to prepare administrators for troubled times.

1

Introduction: A New Profession and a New Textbook Literature

Thomas Glass

THE PROFESSION AND THE LITERATURE

Is the practice of a profession significantly influenced by its textbook literature? Is the textbook literature of a profession significantly influenced by professional practice? Or, do both occur simultaneously?

Public school educational administration is a comparatively new profession serving a relatively new social institution. As its history falls within an era of mass publication, its members have had access to numerous textbooks, scholarly books, monographs, research studies, and professional journal articles usable to build and guide practice.

This book addresses the following three important questions:

1. Can the history of educational administration be traced through its literature?
2. What literature has been most influential in establishing norms of practice?
3. Has there been a coherent body of literature sufficient to guide the profession?

This book does not purport to be a textbook of the history of educational administration. Nor does it necessarily discuss the most important literature in the profession. The appropriateness of the literature reviewed or noted will not meet with the approval of all readers. We do not apologize,

1

but instead maintain that a review of texts implies subjective judgments. The book certainly provides a brief snapshot of an important profession and its textbook literature.

A HISTORY OF TEXTBOOK LITERATURE

A body of textbook literature exists for every professional field. Textbooks have historically been important conveyors of knowledge about desirable practices and knowledge deemed essential to professional roles and practice. In some respects a textbook is the bible of a profession. Textbooks used in academic preparation programs have been and are primary tools for socializing initiates to the profession. Textbooks, especially those used in introductory-level courses, often provide novices with a first glimpse of their profession as seen through the eyes of the authors.

Professions such as law, engineering, and medicine have developed an extensive textbook literature continually renewed by updated knowledge. Other professions not so empirically or scientifically anchored develop textbook literature at a slower pace, as knowledge and practice remain static over longer periods of time. An excellent example is the field of educational administration, which has passed through perhaps five identifiable stages of development during the twentieth century.

The use of textbooks in the United States by practicing professional educators and students has been continuous since the beginning of the common school movement in the 1840s. Two of the earliest texts for students were *Pilgrim's Progress* and the *McGuffey's Readers*. These pioneering educational texts supplemented, but did not replace, the Christian Bible in classrooms across the nation in the nineteenth century (Elson, 1964, pp. 18–19).

In early days books were expensive and difficult to obtain. Many schools possessed few and depended on blackboards, hornbooks, and rote learning. With the coming of steam-powered presses and cheaper paper, textbooks became less expensive and were purchased for use in schoolrooms across the nation. By the end of the Civil War, most public school students had access to at least one or two textbooks.

THE PROFESSION OF PREPARING
ADMINISTRATORS

The training of teachers to become principals (school administrators) did not emerge as a nationally recognized profession until the late nineteenth and early twentieth centuries. Consequently, a textbook library on school administration is very limited until well after World War I. Textbooks teaching teachers were more numerous, as "normal school" students needed to be schooled in the craft of teaching. These early texts often provided content knowledge, as well as teaching morals and methodology (Elson, 1964). During the period between 1880 and 1930, teachers and principals (and superintendents) became more numerous and were state licensed and college educated (many teachers trained in two-year "normal" schools).

The rapid growth of school districts in large towns and cities spurred the development of educational-administration preparation programs in higher-education institutions. These new programs were created to instruct the growing number of principals in the city districts. As programs grew at Teachers College, George Peabody College, Stanford University, the University of Chicago, and the University of Wisconsin, a need arose for general textbooks in educational administration.

In the 1920s the first substantial body of textbook literature written specifically for school administrators was well established. Many of its authors were professors of educational administration at leading universities. The early textbook authors were often not only professors, but former superintendents in large urban school districts. Practicing superintendents sometimes were authors and in many cases had been graduate students of the professors writing the first generation of texts.

This led to texts fairly consistent in their content, approach, and goals. The first thirty years of the literature demonstrate a set of common theses regarding the sanctity of American democracy, the Protestant work ethic, and traditional values of virtue and hard work. The organizational context of schools fitting the "American system of education" was borrowed from early twentieth century scientific-management principles.

Perhaps the guiding light for early educational administration was Frederick Taylor's scientific-management theories focused on efficiency and profit. Scientific-management emphases on specialized roles, time orientation, and layered organizations still survive today in the structure and management of public schools. Connectionist theory and emphasis on specialized secondary teaching has been a strong force shaping American secondary school organization that has resisted restructuring (Callahan, 1962).

Running counter to scientific management has been human relations theory (research) developed in the 1930s by Mary Parker Follett and Luther Gulick. Some educational-administration textbook authors adopted this "new" and more humane way of managing schools. Many of these same writers were followers of John Dewey's progressive education movement in classroom teaching and school organization. The practices advocated by the human relations and progressive education schools are found embedded in educational-administration texts of both yesterday and today (Tyack and Hansot, 1982). A study of textbook literature encounters an array of different text content set into a consistent theme of morals and "Americanism." Although dozens of administrative-practice-based "cookbooks" were published between 1920 and 1980, few were anchored in forceful philosophical foundations.

Themes and movements in private-sector management, technology, and academic philosophy have always affected public school leadership. As schools generally reflect the community in which they reside, professionals serving those schools typically align professional practice with the wishes and desires of that community. The influence of the business and professor sectors in many communities undoubtedly has shaped American school management. In the early years this influence was mostly exerted on a local basis. With the growth of media (including professional textbooks), the influence became more national.

The American educational system of local control has worked well in tandem with the state as a distant overseer. The practice of local boards making a majority of local policies has seldom been challenged in the textbook literature. The American school board is a national icon strongly supported throughout history by the American public. Educational-administration textbook authors, while not challenging the authority of boards, labor to "find" practical ways principals and superintendents can "help" and "lead" boards.

EDUCATIONAL ADMINISTRATION
ENTERS A NEW ERA

The behavioral and social sciences after World War II began to exert a strong influence on the field of educational administration and its textbooks. Leading educational-administration professors considered theory and research in these fields to have direct application in administering schools. Soon social and psychological theory and research in human motivation, organizational culture, leadership, and organizational theory appeared in general textbooks. These texts were often authored by professors with academic training in social psychology, sociology, and organizational leadership.

Professors with more traditional academic backgrounds continued publishing texts much like compendiums of best professional practices. These "cookbooks" of best practices learned through experience were perhaps more widely used in former "teacher colleges" than in major research institutions. Until the 1980s this type of text continued to dominate a good portion of the textbook field.

THE THEORY MOVEMENT DEVELOPS AND
CREATES A TWO-TIER BODY OF TEXTS

By the late 1960s a theory movement in educational administration was present in prestigious research institutions sponsoring educational-administration programs. Faculty members like Daniel Griffiths, Andrew Halpin, Jacob Getzels, James Lipman, Robert Owen, and Egon Guba chaired numerous doctoral dissertations of future educational-administration professors. In addition to influencing talented doctoral students, they also wrote extensively. Early on, their efforts turned in the direction of introductory textbooks reflecting social and behavioral science research and theory. The goal of the new theorists was to develop a unique "theory of educational administration," and what better way to disseminate this theory than in general textbooks? Earlier generations of professors attempted to identify the best practices and trait characteristics of the best leaders.

Now, the new generation of professors went beyond best practices to re-create the administrative role as that of social scientist.

Another goal of the new theory movement in educational administration was to create "professional legitimacy." The theory professors, especially those working in research universities, felt a field-based applied profession like educational administration might only achieve academic respectability if it possessed a unique theory and research base. Another possible objective was the desire on the part of faculty to become more respectable and have an opportunity to move up a notch in the academic pecking order.

Many textbooks were still compendiums of best practices, history, governance, and curriculum leadership. They too were affected by the theory movement and in later editions devoted chapters to leadership, organization, and motivation theory. Even with add-on chapters, they were not pure theory and research texts. Many educational-administration students were never exposed to both schools (practitioner and theory) of educational administration. This might be the point when many educational-administration programs began to distance themselves from practitioners.

From the 1970s through the 1990s, textbooks became very specialized, as did the profession and its textbook authors. Few professors considered themselves generalists in the field. In many departments teaching general courses in educational administration became the least desirable teaching assignment. In some departments adjunct professors often taught the general introductory-level administration course.

Today, educational-administration professors usually identify themselves as belonging to a field such as policy, school law, personnel, business management, finance, facilities, instructional leadership, and organizational theory. The specialization of the professoriate fits classical scientific-management theory. This same scientific-management model is vehemently criticized by these same professors as being bureaucratic and inefficient, and harboring vestiges of the undesirable, unscientific past in educational administration.

NEW PROFESSIONAL ORGANIZATIONS
HELP TEXTS

Professional organizations have always provided a platform for the development of textbooks. In the early part of the twentieth century, administrators dominated the National Education Association (NEA) and its departments serving principals and superintendents. Numerous textbook authors were very active participants in NEA departments. A good number of "administration" books flowed from the output of commissioned studies funded by the NEA. The sharing of professional interests in professional associations with principals, superintendents, and business managers was the early norm. At this point in educational-administration history the interests of the professors and practitioners were closely aligned (Sears, 1946).

By the late 1950s new organizations representing principals and superintendents were established, attracting fewer educational-administration professors as active members. Instead, specialized organizations for educational-administration professors emerged, such as the National Council of Professors of Educational Administration, the University Council on Educational Administration, the American School Finance Association, and Division A (administration) of the American Educational Research Association.

Other specialized organizations serving the professional interests of school-law professors, school-finance professors, school-community-relations professors, and school-facility-planning professors appeared during the 1960s. With the rapid expansion of specialized organizations, few professors could remain active in both generalist practitioner organizations and those in their academic specialty. Left far behind in professor membership were professional organizations serving practitioners. This was another sign of the widening breach between professors and practitioners.

The effect of specialized fields has led to a professoriate separated into special-interest groups. The school-law professors typically have little interest in the work of school-finance professors, and both groups have little in common with instructional-leadership focused professors. This splintering creates a dearth of professors seeing the total picture of the practice of school administration. Each professor knows a great deal about a piece of the puzzle, but lacks a broader perspective as to how their piece fits with other pieces. In brief, few visualize what the picture on the jigsaw puzzle box looks like or how all the pieces fit together. This splintering has resulted in a plethora of specialized textbooks featuring a narrow focus on just one area of school administration. Sometimes these texts overlap, conflict, and create a confused picture for students.

THE TEXTBOOK FUTURE IS BACK TO THE PAST

The twenty-first century brings a new movement to standardize preparation and practice in educational administration. In the 1990s sets of professional standards were developed to serve as state-licensing requirements. Instead of bringing unity to the field, they have further split it into specialties addressing specific standards. Soon after the standards were published, textbooks appeared, focusing on content and activities needed to verify or satisfy a standard.

Organizations sponsoring standards like the Interstate School Leader Licensing Consortium (ISLLC) and the National Policy Board on Education Administration did so with a minimum of research and field testing. The standards really are sets of guidelines featuring numerous indicators that do not lend themselves to measurement. Unfortunately, they are not standards of practice validated by extensive research on effective practice. In time they may become validated professional standards, but it is likely that a new wave of educational trends (or fads) or political needs will push them into obscurity.

Ironically, the current standards movement is forcing many educational-administration professors back to textbook compendiums of best practices. Several newer casebooks really are cookbooks for practicing and meeting standards at the same time. The standards and indicators align with a theory base in several disciplines. However, the licensing and instructional emphasis is on "how to," not necessarily "why."

The age of standards is affecting newer editions of general texts and creating a market for casebooks that provide practice cases and accompanying suggestions to meet standards. One purpose of these texts is to provide students with experiences in case resolution aligned to the Educational Testing Service–developed written examination required for administrator licensing in many states. Some professors argue that the standards movement is an excellent example of "dumbing down" preparation programs. This may or may not be true.

The view that a set of general professional standards can adequately serve all administrators in all types of districts is highly questionable. Current administrator-preparation programs and textbooks are content-specific, assuming the district possesses an administrator for personnel, finance, curriculum, remedial education, special education, and support services. In reality a minority of school districts employ a full complement of specialized educational administrators. The average American school district has about twenty-four hundred students (Glass, Bjork, and Brunner, 2000).

Interestingly, both states and professional organizations sponsoring standards do not differentiate between the principalship and the superintendency, despite enormous differences, well verified by research, between the two positions. Also, important operational differences affecting practice exist in district size, client groups, educational programs, and communities. Relatively few text writers after 1960 have noticed and acknowledged practice differences between large and small districts. Since the 1970s texts have appeared on administering urban schools, but they differ little from other texts, with the exception of using the word "urban."

Another interesting paradox exists in texts on principalship. Until the 1980s principalship texts were written for either elementary or secondary principals. Later texts address the concept of "the principalship," even though the secondary and elementary principalships have become more dissimilar than similar. The same generalizing is true for the few textbooks focusing on the superintendency. It is unclear whether this generalizing of the principalship has been the result of authors' or publishers' attempts to capture a wider market.

CRITICAL THEORY AND POSTMODERNISM: AFFECT ON TEXTS

As social and behavioral theory has faded to a degree from professorial attention, the void has been partially filled by postmodernism and critical theory. Their advocates proclaim a new reality for schooling and its role in society. Their view of the future is clear, but the paths to get there are vague at best. These writers appear to be caught in the dilemma of using critical theory to achieve a new society in an era of ever-increasing conservatism. The effect of postmodernist thought on the preparation of administrators will likely be minimal as a sizable majority of principals and superintendents are being certified in traditionally conservative second-tier institutions that are not research oriented. Although the publishing market is full of academic books on critical theory and postmodernism, there are very few textbooks showing how to practice their ideology.

What might be the future of textbooks in educational administration? It is an ominous sign that more and more professors are using trade books as textbook adoptions in many general and specialized courses. Most come from the private sector and reflect a current hot topic. In the 1980s and early 1990s, some of these topics included total quality management as advocated by the Japanese, learning organizations, transformational leadership, effective habits of effective leaders, and bottom-up management. These hot topic books are heavily marketed by megabookstores and private-sector consultants who appear frequently at education meetings and conferences. Most of these books are available in reasonably priced paperback editions. They feed the historical practice of administrators and professors of jumping on private-sector bandwagons. The management gurus all sell expensive, cure-all silver bullets.

Many current general school-administration texts are aligned with specialist texts. For instance, chapters on curriculum, school law, finance, and personnel prepare students for later specialized courses and textbooks. This preparation is made more difficult by using books borrowed from the private sector. The historical game of guarding turf in higher education aside, the question arises, if there is no need for an education-based text, is there a need for the course? If there is no education content, why not teach the course in another department or college?

TEXTBOOKS, PUBLISHERS, AND COSTS

The high cost of hard- and softcover texts is another factor influencing the text adoptions of many professors. A general textbook and a casebook cost between $75 and $125. If a student takes two graduate courses, the costs of texts might be half that of tuition. Publishers attribute the high textbook prices to a limited sales market. This is somewhat difficult to believe when many popular general and specialized texts are in their third or fourth editions. Also, the production costs of many texts have been shifted offshore to Asia.

A good general textbook describes the pieces of the puzzle and fits them altogether for the benefit of a reader new to a professional occupation. There are likely a few generalist professors remaining who are able to write a comprehensive generalist text. The lack of contemporary and new generalized texts may be a harbinger of the future of educational administration. The professoriate is definitely aging, and many administrator practitioners see an unattractive future for themselves in higher education, featuring low salaries, politics, and remoteness from the field of practice. In the early days the relationship between textbooks, authors, and practice in the field was reciprocal. The writers of the texts were scholar practitioners. In recent decades the writers have principally been academics.

SUMMARY

The fate and future of textbook literature in educational administration are hinged to many factors, such as state licensing requirements, educational-program accreditation, publishing-company bottom lines, the academic abilities and inclinations of professors, and the actual survival of the discipline as an identifiable field of study.

REFERENCES

Callahan, R. (1962). *The cult of efficiency.* Chicago: University of Chicago Press.

Elson, R. M. (1964). *Guardians of tradition.* Lincoln: University of Nebraska Press.

Glass, T. E., Bjork, L., and Brunner, C. (2000). *The study of the American school superintendency: a look at the superintendent in the new millennium.* Arlington: American Association of School Administrators.

Sears, J. (1946). *Cubberley of Stanford.* Palo Alto: Stanford University Press.

Tyack, D. B., and Hansot, E. (1982). *Managers of virtue.* New York: Basic Books.

2

From Idea to Ideology:
School-Administration Texts, 1820–1914

Robert Mason

School administration was clearly recognized as a special function early in the nineteenth century. New York State established the office of state superintendent of common schools in 1812, and Maryland, Illinois, Vermont, Louisiana, Pennsylvania, Michigan, and Kentucky created similar offices before 1840. More than twenty cities had established the office of city superintendent of schools by the end of the Civil War. A national association of school superintendents was formed in 1865, and this organization became the Department of Superintendence of the NEA a few years later. Nevertheless, duties and prerogatives of school management remained quite diffuse and inconsistent from situation to situation, and individuals holding office as superintendents did not always possess the power to manage school affairs. Few cities designated the school superintendent as the chief executive of the board in the nineteenth century. For example, there is the statement of record outlining the duties of the superintendent of schools in Boston in 1859 (Annual Report of the School Committee of the city of Boston, 1959). Section 6 of that document obligates the superintendent of schools to "consult with the different bodies who have control of the building and altering of school houses" and "advise" concerning appropriations and expenditures. But his functions bearing upon fiscal matters are strictly limited to "consultation," "communication," "suggestion," and "advisement."

CITY SCHOOLS

City schools in other parts of the nation developed as they had been established in rural areas. Voters in a ward voted to have a school; the ward

13

became a school district; and each ward school was managed as an autonomous institution. Even city school boards functioned in a decentralized manner prior to urban school reforms in the late 1800s (Cronin, 1973, p. xxi).

In a very real sense, schools, thus managed, were people's institutions, set up, controlled, and financed by nonprofessionals. Teachers were hired to exercise an expertise that did not extend beyond that of the best-educated parents in the community. Not all people in the community possessed the expertise of the teacher, but they were sufficiently familiar with it not to be overawed. Thus, teachers were hired to keep school and hear pupils recite from books with which at least some of the parents were familiar. Teachers, that is, were dealing with familiar materials and skills. Thus, it also becomes understandable that school administrators were sometimes charged only with menial maintenance duties. At other times, they were expected to do everything from supervising a spelling bee to fixing a leaky faucet. In general, they were most responsible for the supervision of the instructional program, and as the years went by, this became the predominant way in which their time was spent. Many school boards hired a separate person to purchase school supplies and to be in charge of the school facilities (Reller, 1941, p. 8).

SCHOOL ADMINISTRATION
BECOMES MORE ACADEMIC

As school administration became increasingly professional toward the end of the nineteenth century, a shift toward academics was definitely visible. School administrators worked to get more power in selecting teachers, supervising instruction, examining pupils, and releasing fiscal management to the board. Generally, before the turn of the century, administrators did not seek fiscal responsibility or power, as this was exercised directly by the board, in some instances through a full-time business manager appointed by the board or chosen in the same way the members of the board were chosen. This official frequently outranked the superintendent by virtue of his prior appointment to the position and his prerogative to make recommendations to the board concerning appointments to the office of superintendent. No mention is found of a converse relationship entailing either the right or obligation of an incumbent superintendent to make recommendations to the board concerning a vacancy in the office of business manager. The superintendent had no fiscal responsibility and no prerogatives in the management of school business. He was an officer subordinate to the business executive and communicated with the board on financial and plant management matters through him only. He was, however, directly responsible for the academic or instructional activities—textbooks, courses of study, teaching methods, progress of pupils. Appointment of teachers was a moot point. However, the Committee of Fifteen recommended that he be given independent power to appoint and assign from an "eligible list" and to discontinue services for cause at his discretion (NEA, 1895, pp. 375–397).

By the late nineteenth century, it was generally agreed among educators that two offices were necessary, one for the administration of business affairs, the other for instruction. Among educators there was almost unanimous agreement that administration should be separated into two "great" independent departments (NEA, 1895). As a result, the superintendent and not the business officer began to emerge as the chief executive officer of school districts (Reller, 1935, p. 281).

In 1895, the Committee of Fifteen further recommended that the management of the business interests of a city school system and the supervision of instruction should be formally separated. The business executive was to be elected in the same manner as members of the board or appointed by the board prior to the appointment of a superintendent of instruction. The superintendent of instruction, it was recommended, should be board appointed upon nomination by the business executive. In concert with this recommendation, the Department of Superintendence of the National Education Association endorsed the Cleveland Plan, according to which an elected school director would serve as chief executive of the school system responsible for overall direction and business management. This elected official would select a superintendent of instruction.

Thus, only after 1900 did professional school administration become a field invested with the power of office. Earlier, school administration was a matter of assigning and guiding pupils as approved by the board, supervising teachers appointed by the board, and developing courses of study related to any approved and adopted textbooks. So, administration and teaching were not sharply separated; schools were "kept," not really administered, and educators of vision gained whatever power they had by hard work, persuasion, and charisma, rather than by virtue of their positions. Nevertheless, a manual of practice did develop during the nineteenth century, laying the groundwork for today's profession of school administration. To inquire into the content and perspective of this manual, ten education books published between 1829 and 1908 were examined:

Samuel R. Hall. (1829). *Lectures on School-Keeping.* Boston: Richardson, Lord, and Holbrook.

Samuel R. Hall. (1832). *Lectures to Female School Teachers on School-Keeping.* Boston: Richardson, Lord, and Holbrook.

David A. Page. (1885). *Theory and Practice of Teaching.* New York: A. S. Barnes.

William H. Payne. (1875). *Chapters on School Supervision.* Cincinnati: Wilson, Hinkle, and Co.

William H. Payne. (1901). *Education of Teachers.* New York: B. J. Johnson.

Preston V. Search. (1901). *An Ideal School.* New York: Appleton

Samuel T. Dutton. (1903). *School Management.* New York: Scribner's.

William E. Chancellor. (1915). *Our Schools: Their Administration and Supervision.* 2nd ed. Boston: Heath.

William E. Chancellor. (1907). *A Theory of Motives, Ideals, and Values in Education.* Boston: Houghton Mifflin.

Samuel T. Dutton and David A. Snedden. (1908). *The Administration of Public Education in the United States.* New York: Macmillan.

Distinctions of some importance are made in the analysis to follow between Dutton's book on school management, published in 1903, and Dutton and Snedden's text on school administration, issued in 1908. Therefore, a reference to "Dutton" is to be taken as pointing only to the 1903 work, while "Dutton and Snedden" will indicate reference to the 1908 book. References to Payne will point to the 1875 book, unless specific mention is made of the work he wrote twenty-five years later, after he had become associated with George Peabody College. The ten volumes listed are, thus, reduced to seven authors, to be identified chronologically as follows:

Hall: 1829
Page: 1847
Payne: 1875
Search: 1901
Dutton: 1903
Chancellor: 1904
Dutton and Snedden: 1908

EDUCATION, PIETY, COMMON SENSE, AND MANAGEMENT

Thus designated, Hall, Page, and Payne express an emphasis on order, piety, and humane nineteenth-century values, untouched by science, but full of wonderful common sense. Dutton presents a compendium broken down into an almost overwhelming array of didactic specifications for school management (Dutton, 1903). This work is an example of professional self-consciousness, neither effete nor exaggerated, but arising out of meticulous notation and classification of the array of tasks involved in running schools. Yet this work remains untouched by theory, comprehensive survey of practices, or controlled experimentation. It is a work not to be ridiculed or taken lightly, a practical handbook, a comprehensive how-to manual.

If I find the arguments of our professional ancestors hilariously funny, I intend no disrespect to their memory; Chancellor can be nominated as the Lord Pooh-Bah of the group. He thunders from a mountain midway between Olympus and Ararat, frequently defending his pronouncements with the sort of impeccable idealistic logic that might be called "horse sense made asinine." The utter finality of his statements is overwhelming, and they are occasionally beautifully quotable. I think the following is a poignant "Chancellorism": "Sex is a matter of indifference, except so far as salary is concerned" (Chancellor, 1915, p. 211).

Search's 1901 book and the Dutton and Snedden volume of 1908 cross the threshold into twentieth-century educational science. The one, written by a former student and ardent disciple of C. Stanley Hall, foreshadows the transformation of educational theory, if not the widespread practice represented by the early progressives, in the genre of John and Evelyn

Dewey's *Schools of Tomorrow* (1914). Search makes more administrative sense than the others because he wrote as an experienced school superintendent and insisted that his proposals had specific tryouts in practice. I had never heard of Preston Search until several references led to him. Inasmuch as the progressive education movement has been a major scholarly interest of mine for a good many years, it strikes me that Search may be a lost jewel. Surely *An Ideal School* (1901) deserves attention from those who continue to examine the ideological sources of the New Education. His plan for educational parks sounds exactly like what Sidney Harland recommended for Pittsburgh in the mid-1960s. Search insists that transportation problems can be solved if the school schedule is set in concert with city transportation authorities to coincide with the highest off-peak periods of the city transit systems.

The other modern work, Dutton and Snedden (1908), is in the science-of-education style of Strayer and Thorndike, to be distinguished from the developmental-psychological emphasis of Hall and the child-centered school movement (Dutton and Sneeden, 1908). A good many of Dutton's cookbook recipes remain in, but at least one-third of this six-hundred-page textbook in school administration is systematic survey and description of well-established practices in social context. Clearly implicit is the assumption that best practice arises out of knowledge of the range of practice currently in vogue. Here we have the beginnings of the notion that the inductive compilation of current instances is the stuff out of which improved policy and practice can be elicited. The survey method, but nothing approaching experimentation, is represented.

Such a grouping of the ten books and seven authors consulted can be captioned as follows:

Group A. Mid-century works based in the accepted nineteenth-century worldview and established notions of the good life (Hall, Page, and Payne)

Group B. A practical compendium of recommended best practices grounded in practical common sense and personal experience (Dutton)

Group C. Nineteenth-century philosophical idealism worked out in an agenda for school administration (Chancellor)

Group D. A foreshadowing of the child-centered school emphasis in progressive education (Search)

Group E. A foreshadowing of the science-of-education movement (Dutton and Snedden)

A QUEST FOR ORDER

A constant theme of the early books is the necessity of order. Hall develops the argument of the utilitarians that order is a necessity for happiness (Hall, 1829, p. 73). Page insists "it is a law of our being that we can do well but one thing at a time" (Page, 1847, p. 202). Payne argues that inasmuch as tasks must be ordered according to "firstness," "secondness," "thirdness," and so on, execution of a plan for dealing with the tasks demands an ordering of lines of authority (Payne, 1875, p. 13). Thus, he establishes the necessity, laid down as a rule, that a school system be directed by one responsible head (Payne, 1875, p. 17). Page in 1847 and Payne in 1875 develop in strongly explicit detail an analysis of lines of authority, delegation, and sovereignty from the people to the board, to superintendents and principals, and to teachers (Page, 1847, p. 364). Powers delegated to the board by the people and to the superintendent by a board are irrevocable during the contractual time specified, unless the individuals are removed from office by impeachment. The people, by electing school trustees or a school committee, delegate to them power to manage the school, thereby investing them with the responsibility to do so. The board delegates specified duties to the superintendent, thereby investing him in turn with rights and responsibilities, and he in turn delegates responsibilities to his subordinates, the teachers.

At each level, sovereignty is delegated and, once this has been done, is not to be infringed upon or withdrawn, except in instances of such gross abuse as justify impeachment. To support such an arrangement, prerogatives at each level must be specified as clearly as possible, with individuals, then, remaining free from interference in exercising their prerogatives. Page does not distinguish between superintendents and principals, using the terms interchangeably in his 1847 book. But Payne, a quarter of a century later, treats the principal as a part-time administrator subordinate to the superintendent in his administrative role, but holding the status of teacher. Thus, Payne does not provide for clear sovereignty delegated from superintendent to principal, treating the latter as a staff position.

Payne's extension of the argument of delegated sovereignty to teachers is strong and uncompromising. The administrator should trust his teachers, giving them freedom to follow their own methods of instruction and discipline within very broad general guidelines. His record of teacher evaluations should be limited to a half-dozen general criteria such as "order," "manner," "skill in instruction," and "discipline." Page and Payne set a high standard indeed of academic freedom and responsibility for teachers; the most uncompromisingly ardent devotee of academic freedom in our own day could scarcely ask for more. Both Page and Payne lay great stress upon the need for clarity and precision in specifications as to what is delegated at each stage, urging that lack of clarity can bring down the whole structure of delegated powers.

They were, indeed, in their day, male chauvinists. Hall includes sections on goals and purposes of schools, qualifications and responsibilities of teachers, and public relations in his 1829 book (Hall, 1829). Notably missing, however, from the 1832 volume directed explicitly to women primary teachers keeping the summer schools are comments on goals, purposes, and public relations (Hall, 1832). It deals only with the specifics of classroom procedures. Page uses the masculine pronoun throughout, and in the many examples and illustrations, the teacher is always portrayed as a man (Page, 1847). However, Payne's detailed discussion of whether women should be school administrators presupposes full admission and participation by women in teaching jobs (Payne, 1875, p. 46). On the issue discussed, however, Payne concludes that the position of chief school executive should be reserved for men, for at this level "there is need of that judicial firmness which is characteristic of man's nature" (p. 48).

ADMINISTRATION AND THE COMMUNITY

The importance of community and public relations is stressed by all three of the mid-century authors, with Hall's discussion coming closest to our contemporary view of public relations. The importance of schooling is to be made apparent to parents by clear statements of what schools can and cannot do. An essential of good public relations is clear and forceful presentation of the goals of the school and the argument that these goals are worthy of benevolent public support. Thus may the educator cut through community religious and political difference to present the school's case. He advises, "You must be prepared to govern your scholars at school, and *may* often find it necessary to exert nearly as much influence with *parents* as with them" (Hall, 1829, p. 44).

Page advises that explicit disciplinary problems in school may be the reflection of community differences of opinion and factionalism among the parents. Evenhandedness by the teacher in and out of school must be the watchword, but the teacher must, in any case, establish order in school, by corporal punishment if necessary (Page, 1847, p. 243). He frowns upon expulsion as legally moot and probably inexpedient (p. 248). Visits to the district by the teacher before the school term opens, along with visits to homes, both wealthy and poor, are advised, and parents should be encouraged to visit school throughout the year (p. 264). The teacher should get to school early on the first day so as to meet the pupils one by one as they arrive. Yet, the progression must be from informality to order; the objective is the ordering of activities (Payne, 1843). Payne advocates forming lay committees to visit the schools and file written reports.

Deep moral dedication is expected of the nineteenth-century educator. Teaching is viewed by Hall as an occupation demanding total dedication, pursued under the eye of a Creator-God and Heavenly Father to whose glory the enterprise must be fully dedicated (Hall, 1929, p. 48). A teacher is "doing his Heavenly Father's business" (Page, 1847, p. 401). Teaching is a "spiritual art" (p. 72).

The emphasis on order and ordering as a very condition of rationality, hence fundamental to school organization, has been pointed out in the mid-century works. Dutton's *School Management* (1903) might be read as the epitome of this emphasis collated in a textbook. Dutton, professor of school administration at Teachers College, Columbia University, alleges, "school management, broadly speaking, relates to the conditions affecting the school, as well as to everything that takes place there" (Dutton, 1903, p. 3). This book by Dutton is like a handbook on formal landscape gardening. The end product is a vision of orderly beauty. Total effect is the end concern. But to achieve this effect, meticulous attention to the smallest detail is demanded. This work of 275 pages includes recommendations for specific lesson outlines, placement and design of cloakrooms (to be partitioned off with wire mesh for better ventilation and drying of clothing in wet weather), and a discourse on the Herbartian doctrine of the five formal steps. Specifically theological allusions do not appear in this work, but the moral ordering of the human person is the educational objective. Finally, external motivations are to be discarded as the training and discipline of the school contribute to growth toward maturity. Thus, by the ministrations of the orderly school, "the personality is trained, disciplined, and brought nearer to perfection" (Dutton, 1909, p. 3).

Chancellor was superintendent of public instruction of the District of Columbia and lectured on education at Johns Hopkins and George Washington University, later becoming a professor of political science at the College of Wooster. In his thinking, the emphasis on order, orderliness, and ordering becomes a part of an explicit and consistent moral idealism. Thus, Chancellor's writing combines a somewhat pompous morality with didactic practical maxims.

THE WISDOM OF CHANCELLOR

Chancellor makes a good many references to school finance and the need for more adequate financial support for schools. He sees the school administrator as a kind of moral or spiritual guide bringing higher culture to the people. The school administrator is subject to citizens and his board, like the Protestant minister, but the minister's sources of wisdom and insight are from on high. "The school is a temple of learning, the shrine of progress. Positive philanthropy is its sacred mission" (Chancellor, 1907, p. 29).

Board members, teachers, and administrators are to be people of highest character devoted wholeheartedly to the public good. The superintendent is their moral mentor, responsible to them, yet always representing before them the model of firm and unswerving righteousness. This entire work is didactic; Chancellor pronounces and proclaims the truth. Tuesday is the best day in the week for the board meeting. The payroll for 1,000 pupils in small communities should be $60,000 (Chancellor, 1907, p. 160). There are twelve basic principles of sound school administration (p. 88). Other examples of Chancellor's wisdom include the following:

1. "Women generally have greater difficulty in persuading boys over thirteen years of age to sing than men have, while girls of any age are easily led to sing by either men or women. Consequently, in high school, a man teaching singing is preferable" (Chancellor, 1907, p. 211).
2. Regarding textbook agents, "the superintendent should welcome their coming and speed their going" (p. 168).
3. "The superintendent has a certain relation to former board members, especially to those who are strong supporters of his policy" (p. 164).
4. "The relation of the superintendent to 'reformers' is sometimes one of special difficulty" (p. 187).

Lest Chancellor's pomposity be construed as totally conservative, however, it is important to note his extreme strictures upon controls over education exercised by business and the state. He deplores state education for citizenship as much as he deplores the pressure of business interests upon schools (Chancellor, 1903, p. 43). The primary tasks of education as a formal system are to maintain the aristocracies of talent, to identify the best children of the masses, to elevate these children of talent and ability into the vacant places in the aristocracy, and to prepare the masses for routine work and submission to the direction of the aristocracy. But Chancellor makes clear that he is not speaking of an aristocracy of blood or material inheritance (p. 92).

Chancellor's democratic view is that "Education is nothing but religion enlightened and energized, but always and essentially the religion of the faith that all are the sons of God, and that as long as He lives even the worst may be redeemed" (Chancellor, 1903, p. 111).

Such education—education as it ought to be—is not exemplified by educational institutions in America. The public schools, in particular, are subordinate to other institutions, especially the state and business. Thus, the fundamental thrust of Chancellor's argument becomes how to bring about true education, which means rescuing the schools from the debilitating control of the political and economic establishment. Far from subsuming the task of schools to the service of business and industry, Chancellor equates efficiency with intellectual power. He states, "Efficiency is making something worthwhile . . . efficiency is the health of the will."

He writes, "Mere doing is not efficiency. The doing must be intelligent, purposeful doing of things worthwhile. Therefore, in a high civilization, the greatest efficiency is the accomplishment of a generous intelligence, yet such intelligence is in itself not enough; it is merely the condition of efficiency" (p. 243). Business and war are inherently immoral. Ideals that are the proper concern of the school are the intelligence, efficiency, and morality; those of the university are science, art, and philosophy. The school is concerned with education, the university with culture (Chancellor, pp. 310–328). The dedication of both the school and the university must be to health and holiness (p. 385). All school and university studies should finally be evaluated according to their contribution to these criteria: intelligence, efficiency, morality, science, art, philosophy, health, and holiness.

Chancellor thinks of the natural human being uninfluenced by education as savage, the city dweller as barbaric. Cities are necessary for manufacturing, but people cannot make their homes in cities. People are to live in hamlets and villages built solely for habitation. The open country is for forestry and agriculture, but not for habitation. Cities will be for manufacture, mining, and trade, but not for habitation (Chancellor, p. 460).

Education is not induction into conformity with the conventions and ideals of society; it is not adjustment to civilization. Unlike education as proposed in Dewey's *Democracy and Education* (1916), it is the discovery of the deepest realities of the soul, which lie nearest to the source whence all souls spring (p. 465).

In Chancellor's ideal society dedicated to the good, lay boards of control for educational affairs will be done away with, and the public will control only financial issues. Churches, schools, and the government itself will be staffed by professionals (p. 479).

SEARCH, DUTTON, AND SNEDDEN AND POLICY IN THE TWENTIETH CENTURY

If Chancellor is taken to exemplify the continuing influence of Victorian high idealism on American schools at the turn of the century, we may construe Search (1901) and Dutton and Snedden (1908) as foreshadowing the course of American educational policy during the first half of the twentieth century. For, with the exception of the back-to-the-liberal-arts movement led by Hutchins and taking place mainly during the World War II years, policy arguments between 1900 and 1950 were most strongly influenced by the conflicting claims of the child-centered school and the science-of-education movement. Preston W. Search's *Ideal School* (1901), inspired by G. Stanley Hall, not Dewey, is a good example of the former (Search, 1901).

Search, who studied at Clark University, published this book in 1901, after having served as a superintendent of schools in Ohio; Colorado; Los Angeles, California; and Holyoke, Massachusetts. William Torrey Harris wrote the preface and G. Stanley Hall an introduction. The book is dedicated to Hall. At the outset, Search specifies that the school must be pupil centered, democratic, and in accord with nature and must conduct its work by the "active method." It must recognize individual differences and do away with all false incentives and extrinsic rewards. Pupils must not be subordinated to the machine. A first mission of the school must be to promote physical health. Search thinks that much nearsightedness and spinal curvature is aggravated by poor school conditions (Search, 1901, p. 102).

Thus, schools must be built to provide much sunshine and light, play, contact with nature, handwork, and physical activity. Campus-type schools are proposed, and several farm schools are described as models. Studios, laboratories, workshops, and gardens should be included. To make such schools financially feasible, they should be located where land is cheaper, away from central cities, but with public transportation readily available. Search would do away with the twelve grades and substitute four departments—play school, elementary school, intermediate school, and high school (p. 95). But schools should be open into the evening hours to provide a full array of community and adult-education services. Appropriate summer activities should continue in the school parks during the summer months.

It seems clear that Search is applying to school planning the full developmental point of view represented by his teacher C. Stanley Hall. But he presents charts and tables of growth rates to support his arguments for individual differences and acknowledges indebtedness to John Dewey's recommendation that "school is to be life" (p. 175). He favors departmentalization of elementary instruction so that children will have contact with several different teachers. Children are to have their own gardens at home, with school time devoted to discussions and plans concerning these gardens. Toads, frogs, and even beehives will be at school from time to time. Formal instruction in reading can wait until children are eight years old. French and German are to be taught by the direct method. Letter grades are to be abolished in favor of ordinary written descriptions of the work accomplished and conferences with parents (p. 213). He thinks it is a good thing for school faculties to be mainly made up of women (p. 302). "The schools will always be taught largely by women, and properly so, because of woman's finer intuitions" (pp. 302–303).

The way to upgrade the school superintendency is to give greater responsibility to those holding the office. Search is less than enthusiastic about teacher tenure. He advocates nonpartisan, staggered elections of school board members, the optimum school board size being five. The board should appoint teachers on the superintendent's recommendation (p. 305).

Surely, Search is a modern for the moderns. He refers specifically to evolution as an accepted phenomenon of nature, and there are no religious allusions in his book. He recommends physical health, happiness, much activity, constant out-of-door movement, one-story schools full of light and air opening to the outdoors, flexible scheduling, and elimination of letter grades. And he insists, in conclusion, that he is a practical "school man," that his proposals have actually been tried out, that they will work.

Although separated by only five years in publication dates, Dutton's *School Management* (1903) and Dutton and Snedden's *The Administration of Public Education in the United States* (1908) are a full epoch apart in style and impact. Dutton's prescriptions for administrative practice that make up the 1903 book on management are retained, but these are introduced and consistently supported by or related to explicit surveys of contemporary practice and references to surveys of community conditions. The later volume is characterized by conventional textbook trappings. Chapters and subdivisions are clearly captioned and organized, and the first quarter of the six-hundred-page book is devoted to hard empirical survey data of contemporary practice. School finance is given extended treatment, and a separate chapter is devoted to educational statistics. Surely, the great distinction between the two books must be due to the influence of the collaborator.

Snedden was the first in professional education scholarship to bring scientific sociology to bear upon education. Nevertheless, Snedden's sociology, as reflected in *The Administration of Public Education in the United States* (1908), is primitive. It exhibits the methodological presumption that stipulations of best practice are to be grounded in exhaustive enumeration and collation of current actual practices—that you must have detailed knowledge of what's going on before you formulate administrative policy. But the gap from survey of present practice to pronouncement of best policy is not bridged, even as today we frequently leap from norm-referenced to criterion-referenced policy, assuming, in spite of ourselves, that the norm becomes the criterion.

The Dutton and Snedden book of 1908 combines Dutton's ingenious seat-of-the-pants maxims for best practice with Snedden's surveys. They do not show the relationships between the two, however. Their work, like ours today, remains vulnerable to the attacks of philosophical analysts who have insisted that there is a fallacy in moving from the "is" to the "ought."

CONCLUSIONS OF EARLY
SCHOOL ADMINISTRATION

In conclusion, what relationships between findings in this survey and recent published scholarship reflect upon schooling in nineteenth and early twentieth-century America? No explicit support for the revisionist argument that the schools functioned as agencies of capitalist oppression is found. There is overwhelming evidence, however, that the schools did represent the moral values affirmed by the official, standard, or established society. Thus, if the revisionist scholars succeed in demonstrating that the nineteenth-century Establishment exemplified capitalist oppression, their argument will hold, by extension, for the schools. It is abundantly clear that the schoolmen did not kowtow explicitly to those in positions of political and economic power; their dedication was to righteousness and purity, and they took strong and courageous positions, insisting that schools were not to be subverted to control by special interests. The revisionists cannot show explicit subservience of the schoolmen to the Establishment; their argument must rest primarily on showing that the capitalist mentality was implicit in the Christian-idealist moral code of the social order of the time. In this connection, it is to be noted that Chancellor, who in so many ways epitomizes the caricatured nineteenth-century idealist, takes a position worthy of Paul Goodman in deploring the control of schools by politicians and businessmen.

As for Tyack's impressively documented and beautifully expressed argument that the schoolmen of this earlier period were driven by the vision of perfection, this small study supports the position fully (Tyack, 1974). They believed in the true, the good, and the beautiful and considered that all human beings are perfectible toward the *summum bonum*. Thus, they did, indeed, assume as a constant the possibility of one best system, and all their efforts were devoted to this end. The possibility of educational pluralism does not even occur to them, as if "multicultural education" would be an obvious and blatant contradiction in terms.

This being the case, Cronin's excoriation of the takeover by the schoolmen when they became powerful enough is supported (Cronin, 1973, p. 57). But a judgment made by Cronin that might well be examined for its grounds is that the "tiny minority of owners and college graduates who wanted the schools to preserve and protect their way of life" were guilty of narrow self-interest (p. 58). This might be extremely difficult to support, for the feature of the nineteenth-century outlook that gave it its greatest strength was its universal humanism. All children, including those of the immigrants, were children of God, subject to his universal law, and perfectible in his image. Nonsectarian schools avoided sectarian interpretations of this worldview only to make possible its full and explicit propagation in the schools. And when the schoolmen took over from the ward bosses, it was because they thought ward politics interfered with the great crusade to extend the vision of the good to every child.

The habit of downgrading the moral idealism of our forebears is so ingrained that what has been just suggested verges on the apparently maudlin or ridiculous. But there is not a shred of evidence in the books examined of an explicit sellout by schoolmen to a business-industrial model of economic efficiency. This sampling would suggest that if that sellout occurred, it happened after 1908. Indeed, it would be entirely in order to extend the sampling. It is also within the realm of possibility that the nineteenth- and early-twentieth-century schoolmen had glimpsed the beatific vision that St. Thomas Aquinas taught was the joint product of faith and reason at work.

REFERENCES

Boston School Committee. (1859). *Annual report.* Boston: Author.

Chancellor, W. E. (1903). *Our schools: their administration and supervision.* Boston: Heath.

Chancellor, W. E. (1907). *Theory of motives, ideals, and values in education.* Boston: Houghton Mifflin.

Cronin, J. (1973). *The control of urban schools: perspective on the power of educational reformers.* New York: Free Press.

Dewey, J., and Dewey, E. (1915). *Schools of tomorrow.* New York: E. P. Dutton.

Dewey, J. (1916). *Democracy and education.* New York: Macmillan.

Dutton, S. T. (1909). *School management.* New York: Scribner's.

Dutton, S. T., and Snedden, D. A. (1908). *The administration of public education in the United States.* New York: Macmillan.

Hall, S. R. (1829). *Lectures on school keeping.* Boston: Richardson, Lord, and Holbrook.

Hall, S. R. (1832). *Lectures to female teachers on school keeping.* Boston: Richardson, Lord, and Holbrook.

National Education Association. (1895). *Journal of proceedings and addresses.* Washington: NEA.

Page, D. P. (1885). *Theory and practice of teaching.* New York: A. S. Barnes.

Payne, W. H. (1875). *Chapters on school supervision.* Cincinnati: Wilson, Hinkle, and Co.

Payne, W. H. (1901). *Education of teachers.* Richmond: B. F. Johnson.

Reller, T. L. (1935). *The development of the city superintendency of schools in the United States.* Philadelphia: Author.

Reller, T. L. (1941). Superintendents of schools. Duties and responsibilities. In Monroe, W. S. (ed.). *Encyclopedia of educational research.* New York: Macmillan.

Search, P. V. (1901). *An ideal school.* New York: Appleton.

Tyack, D. B. (1974). *The one best system: a history of American urban education.* Cambridge: Harvard University Press.

3

From Ideology to Conventional Wisdom: School-Administration Texts, 1915–1933

William Eaton

In the decade between 1901 and 1911, education emerged as a true profession. The struggle to achieve this professionalization had extended back for about seventy-five years when such New England schoolmen as James Carter, Horace Mann, Henry Barnard, and William Russell first began to write and talk about the day when teachers would be trained, when schools would be satisfactorily equipped and financed, when curricula would be planned, and when a body of principles concerning the science of pedagogy would be clearly elucidated. While the details of what happened between 1901 and 1911 to complete the evolution of the profession are beyond the scope of this chapter, suffice it to say that among the factors were the establishment of strong professional associations, the existence of influential periodicals, stronger certification provisions, the beginnings of graduate instruction in professional education, the school survey and standardization movement, and the systematic publication of textbooks that would not only enumerate the principles of education in general, but divide the field into specializations, each of which was beginning to build a base of empirically verifiable data. It is this last factor that is the focus of this chapter.

When Paul Monroe published the influential *Cyclopaedia of Education* in 1911, he mentioned in the introduction that of 8,745 new books issued in the United States in 1910, 348 were new titles in education (Monroe, 1911, p. xi). An analysis of the books published in this era reveals that the two educational specialties most written about were the history of education and educational administration. Of these two, the titles in administra-

31

tion, which includes supervision, certainly dominate in terms of quantity, if not quality. Who wrote these books on school administration? Was it the successful practitioners such as Harris of St. Louis, Gove of Denver, Young of Chicago, or Maxwell of New York? The answer to the question is generally no. The educational-administration books published just prior to 1915 were written by education professors. These professors can be grouped into two camps—those from Teachers College and those from a number of regional teachers colleges. The vital difference between the two is that the authors from Teachers College were attempting to establish their generalizations upon some kind of evidence scientifically gleaned, while most of the authors at the various regional teachers colleges were preparing books for largely local consumption with the more traditional style of basing theories upon personal experience, common sense, and an occasional quote from one of the grand masters, such as Horace Mann or William Torrey Harris.

Prior to 1875 it didn't make sense to talk about school administration; that occupation employed such a small number of people, a separate literature was unnecessary. Between 1875 and 1900, however, the growth in the number of positions of superintendent and full-time principal was spectacular and signaled the need for special training and the textbooks that such training would require. The modern textbook in school administration was a product of the early twentieth century, and the book deserving recognition as the first was Samuel Train Dutton's *School Management: Practical Suggestions Concerning the Conduct and Life of the School*, published by Scribner's in 1903. The book, though it does not use footnotes, does credit the authors it quotes. In this, and in several other ways, it can be regarded as a transitional book bridging the texts of the old and new eras. Like texts of the nineteenth century, it often falls back upon unproven axioms and moralistic judgments. But it represents the modern era by defining the roles of both superintendent and principal and offers a task analysis of their respective roles. Though recognizing the need for efficiency, Dutton rejects the pernicious analogy of the school as a factory. Dutton's book, by admission, is aimed at the big-city school system.

If Dutton's book deserves credit as the first, the credit for the second must go to William E. Chancellor's *Our Schools: Their Administration and Supervision*, published by D. C. Heath in 1904. Chancellor was the superintendent of schools in Bloomfield, New Jersey, which disproves the maxim that practicing administrators were getting out of the business of writing textbooks. Chancellor uses the introduction to his book to justify the need for texts such as his and Dutton's by saying:

> With the growth of our schools in size and in number and with their development in resources and in methods, their organization tends constantly to grow more complex. Recently there has been differentiated from the teachers a class of school directors, administrators, and supervisors, whose function is management rather than instruction. These school managers see the schools from a point of view different from that of the instructors. So recent has been their appearance in the world of education that not only the general public, but even many instructors, do not yet understand the nature and value of their work. To present the subject of American education from the new point of view of the administrator and supervisor is the purpose of this book. (Chancellor, 1904, p. v)

Chancellor did not use any citations or even have a bibliography, so it is impossible to trace his sources. And Chancellor has earned contemporary rancor with his cavalier insistence that women would make bad school board members. He also thought they would make poor administrators on the grounds that if they were mothers they were probably too softhearted, and if they weren't, they were suspect for another set of reasons. It was Chancellor who began the discussion of who makes good and who makes bad board members so characteristic of all of the books in the era of this investigation.

Chancellor's book is written in a straightforward manner. Only twice does he try to dazzle the reader by using Latin or Greek quotations. In the copy examined, Chancellor, while speaking of school boards, said:

> There is a popular idea that, though no one of a dozen men knows much of anything about school teaching, the entire dozen, as a body, has an expert, and therefore a valuable opinion on the subject. This is an interesting aspect of the popular belief in America, *Vox populi, vox dei*. (Chancellor, 1904, p. 49)

A disgruntled student has penned into the margin the following protest: "Speak the American language, you boob!" The use of the Menckenesque word "boob" makes one believe that the protest is itself fifty years old. Chancellor and Dutton set the model for modern books on school administration from 1903 to 1933. Both are widely quoted and frequently cited. But there were other efforts as well.

The Macmillan Company of New York City published a number of important works on education before 1915. In its stable of authors could be found such luminaries as Paul Monroe, Nicholas Murray Butler, William Bagley, Herman Borne, Charles McMurry, Charles DeGarmo, Paul Maims, Edward L. Thorndike, George Strayer, Frank Graves, Samuel Dutton, and David Snedden—a rather formidable array of educational talent. In 1909 Dutton of Teachers College again published an administrative textbook, this time with David Snedden. Their *Administration of Public Education in the United States* was published by Macmillan. A reading of this textbook leaves the reader with the feeling of having just finished a very systematic, very comprehensive, and very boring work. The book's nearly six hundred pages are descriptive, but not prescriptive. The sources used are at least cited, which represents a change from the nineteenth-century practice. It is interesting to note that a large number of citations come from recently completed dissertations done at Teachers College by students such as Elwood P. Cubberley and George D. Strayer. Like other books of its time, Dutton and Snedden's criticizes the large school boards that have dominated in America's large cities, but are already universally condemned for their graft and inefficiency and are in the process of being changed into smaller appointed boards. In reference to school boards, they also address another popular topic—"who makes good board members"—but they speak to the issue in only indirect and polite terms indicating that board members should be honest people of large affairs and should not be compensated for their duties. This latter condemnation of compensation was already the conventional wisdom among schoolmen. Dutton and Snedden's book was aimed at a large national audience, which it reached. Where most of the nineteenth-century books had been regional in character, Dutton and Snedden use studies, statistics, and descriptions from all across the country. Their book has to be recognized as the important standard-bearer of the time.

Also coming out of Teachers College was Strayer and Thorndike's *Educational Administration: Quantitative Studies* published in 1913. Though the book was not written as a primary text in school administration, but rather as a supplement, it deserves recognition not only for the subsequent fame of its authors, but for its heavy emphasis upon establishing an empirical base for the administration of the schools. Again the Teacher College dissertations, which were already being published as the *Teachers College Contributions to Education Series,* provided the numbers that Strayer and Thorndike statistically analyzed. The book has twenty-four chapters that deal with such topics as "Enrollment in Relation to Age and Grade" and "School Achievement in Arithmetic." The book contains 144 full-page statistical tables. This is clearly a break from the nineteenth century. But the biggest break from the past, from my point of view, came with the publication of Ellwood Patterson Cubberley's *Public School Administration* in 1916.

In 1898, Cubberley resigned from a higher-paying job as the superintendent of schools in San Diego to accept a position at the newly founded Leland Stanford Jr. University. Realizing the necessity of obtaining degrees beyond his bachelor's, he left the West Coast during the summer for Teachers College to complete a master's degree in 1902 and a doctorate in 1905. His master's research paper, entitled "Syllabus of Lectures on the History of Education, with Selected Bibliographies and Suggestions As to Reading," was published by Macmillan in 1904. His dissertation, "School Funds and Their Apportionment," did appear in the Contributions Series, but was not commercially published. This was a serious oversight, which Cubberley more than made up for later by using the material in several of his subsequent books. As was mentioned earlier, history and administration were the first two specialties developed within education, and Cubberley was at the forefront of both movements.

From 1909 to 1911 Cubberley worked as a departmental editor for Monroe's *Cyclopaedia of Education,* writing 130 entries for the Cyclopaedia and, in the process, gathering a mass of data. While teaching a summer session at Harvard in 1911, he made the short trip into Boston to visit Houghton Mifflin to propose an educational series under his general editorship. He had already published a book entitled *Changing Conceptions of Education* with the company in 1909 and knew the editors. This latest trip was the birth of the Riverside Series, which ultimately ran to 105 volumes, with Cubberley serving as general editor and personally producing 10 titles for the series. Cubberley's biographers state that the series sold about 3.07 million books and that Cubberley's books accounted for 341,000 of that larger number. Cubberley's ten titles are as follows (Sears and Henderson, 1957, p. 98):

Rural Life and Education (1914)
Public School Administration (1916)
Public Education in the United States (1919)
Readings in the History of Education (1920)
The History of Education (1922)
A Brief History of Education (1922)
The Principal and His School (1923)
An Introduction to the Study of Education and Teaching (1925)
State School Administration (1927)
Readings in Public Education in the United States (1934)

The two most important to school administration were the 1916 *Public School Administration* and the 1923 *The Principal and His School.*

Cubberley, in collaboration with Edward Elliott of the University of Wisconsin, had published their *State and County School Administration* in 1915 with Macmillan. But this was a sourcebook written as a second volume to accompany a principles book that was never published. Cubberley saved his principles for his *Public School Administration,* which was published by Houghton Mifflin the following year.

Cubberley's *Public School Administration,* like Dutton and Snedden's book of seven years earlier, was national in scope and comprehensive in coverage. But unlike Dutton and Snedden's, Cubberley's authoritative voice was prescriptive and not merely descriptive. An analysis of the book's 351 citations reveals that Cubberley's four largest sources of data were the NEA's *Proceedings* (26%); *The Educational Review* (14%); reports from various school surveys (10%); and reports and bulletins of the U.S. Commissioner of Education (9%). These four sources account for about 60 percent of the references listed by Cubberley, the remaining coming from a variety of articles from assorted journals and other textbooks, including Chancellor's and Dutton and Snedden's books. The use of the NEA *Proceedings* and *The Educational Review*—these two sources accounted for 40 percent—provide Cubberley with the force of expert power as he widely quotes the speeches and articles of the nation's big-city school superintendents. Even the annual reports of these superintendents to their respective school boards are quoted not only by Cubberley, but by most textbook authors of the period. William H. Maxwell's *A Quarter Century of Public Development*, published in 1912, is nothing more than excerpts from Superintendent Maxwell's reports to the Brooklyn and then the consolidated New York school boards, plus a few of his NEA addresses.

Cubberley's third major source of information for his *Public School Administration* was that body of literature provided by the fast-growing school-survey movement. Cubberley's significant firsthand knowledge of these surveys came from his being a pioneer in their development and having personally participated in the school surveys of Baltimore, Maryland, in 1911, Portland, Oregon, in 1913, Butte, Montana, in 1914, Oakland, California, and Salt Lake City, Utah, in 1915, Denver, Colorado, in 1916, and the state of New Mexico in 1921. Some of the more important surveys published between 1913 and 1922 (Sears, pp. 429–433) included the following:

Year	Location	Principal Author of Report
1913	Bridgeport, Conn.	James Van Sickle
	New York City	Paul Hanus
1914	Butte, Mont.	B. P. Cubberley
	South Bend, Ind.	Franklin Bobbitt
	Springfield, Ill.	Leonard Ayers
1915	Oakland, Calif.	B. P. Cubberley
	San Antonio, Tex.	Franklin Bobbitt
	Portland, Ore.	E. P. Cubberley
1916	Boston, Mass.	James Van Sickle
	Denver, Colo.	C. H. Judd
	Grand Rapids, Mich.	C. H. Judd
	Salt Lake City, Utah	E. P. Cubberley
1917	Brookline, Mass.	James Van Sickle
	Cleveland, Ohio	Leonard Ayers
	Minneapolis, Minn.	Charles Prosser
	St. Paul, Minn.	Charles Prosser and George Strayer
1918	Gary, Ind.	Abraham Flexner
	Nassau Co., N.Y.	George Strayer
	St. Louis, Mo.	C. H. Judd
1919	State of Maryland	Abraham Flexner
	Memphis, Tenn.	Philander Claxton
	Commonwealth of Virginia	Alexander Inglis

1920	Baltimore, Md.	George Strayer
	Boise, Idaho	Jesse Sears
1921	Arlington, Va.	Jesse Sears
	Atlanta, Ga.	George Strayer and N. L. Engelhardt
	Hackensack, N.J.	George Strayer and N. L. Engelhardt
1922	Augusta, Me.	Alexander Inglis

These surveys provided Cubberley with both numerical data and general principles. The reports and bulletins of the U.S. commissioner were also used for the statistics and the identification of national issues.

Cubberley's *Public School Administration* also deserves credit for being among the first administration textbooks to quote state laws and court cases concerning education. He probably deserves credit for giving birth to the specialization of school law among professors of educational administration. His book *State and County Educational Reorganization: The Revised Constitution and School Code of the State of Osceola*, published by Macmillan in 1914, and his *State and County School Administration* of 1915 had acquainted him with the diverse school laws of the country. From that point on he would make frequent legal citations. But the inclusion of all of these materials still doesn't fully explain why Cubberley's texts were so widely used and critically acclaimed. The reasons for their success are more than just the Cubberley name, for certainly Dutton, Snedden, Strayer, and others enjoyed a high professional reputation as well. The success of Cubberley's administration books is at least fivefold: (1) they were comprehensive and systematic, (2) they were written in an interesting but uncomplicated style, (3) they were authoritative and prescriptive, even "cookbookish," (4) they were immensely practical, and (5) they employed several successful techniques in their format, such as study and discussion questions, numerous charts and graphs, and drawings.

That these books were comprehensive and systematic is easily discovered by a quick perusal of their tables of contents. Cubberley not only identified central administration problems, he generally provided the reader with useful background material to the issues, often of a historical nature. After tracing the evolution of the problem and stating it boldly in contemporary terms, he proceeded with dispatch to solve it before the end of the chapter. Cubberley's style is very straightforward and free from qualifiers and unnecessary adjectives. His prose is also heavily flowered by the epic proportions of "the great struggle to develop common schools" themes so ordinary among all the schoolmen. The common-school quest is the search for the Holy Grail, and the knight in shining armor is the school superintendent or principal, whose purity in the quest for school efficiency and human perfection is not overshadowed by godly Sir Lancelot. Cubberley writes with quiet passion and without artifice.

Certainly Cubberley's books are authoritative and prescriptive. Where others hint, he states. Where others suggest, he insists. Where some leave open for further discussion, he concludes. His books are also very practical. In Cubberley's 1923 *The Principal and His School,* entire chapters are dedicated to the first day of school and how to operate in a crowded building. There are sections on how to run a fire drill and how to supervise the toilets. There are also model forms that can be copied and modified for local use. His references at the ends of chapters are annotated. And lastly, the books have an attractive format and eye appeal; they not only sounded better, they looked better.

The content of Cubberley's *Public School Administration* provides the modern reader with a good idea of the educational issues of seventy years ago. The two pivotal problems for Cubberley were the composition and role of the school board and the qualifications and duties of the school superintendent. The book is unabashedly aimed at the larger city school superintendents and grew out of a course called "City School Administration," which he taught at Teachers College during the summer of 1914. The school board, to Cubberley's mind, should be small, preferably with five to seven members. These members should not receive compensation, or to use his own language, "It may be accepted as a fundamental principle in American educational administration that a school board should not be paid for its services." The school board must also have the right kind of members. Bad board members include teamsters, blacksmiths, young politicians, and cranks with axes to grind. Good board members can be formed from machinists, shoe clerks, real estate agents, druggists, lumberyard foremen, hotel keepers, and old and busy lawyers. In terms of duties, the board should be legislative and not executive in function. Its central job is to hire a good superintendent.

The superintendent should be a man of "strong character, broad sympathies, high purposes, fine culture, courage, exact training, and executive skill" (Cubberly, 1916, p. 131). He should be "clean in mind and body, be temperate in speech and act, be honest and square, have a high sense of personal honor, possess the manners and courtesy of a gentleman, and have a sense of humor" (Cubberly, 1916, p. 135). As he prepares for the responsibilities of a superintendency, he should be willing to move around, and, says Cubberley, "If salary does not seem large enough to cover both married life and study, he should for a time resolutely put marriage aside" (Cubberly, 1916, p. 144). As he goes on to identify the constituent parts of the superintendent's role, it should be noted that Cubberley is not one of those who contributed to the excesses of the school efficiency movement so lucidly described by Raymond Callahan in his 1962 book *Education and the Cult of Efficiency.* To the contrary, he warns the superintendent in his *Principles* to save time for "broad" thinking and to avoid spending too much time on any one thing, such as "bills and supplies, and the general routine work of a business clerk" (pp. 217–218). This theme is continued in his *The Principal and His School,* where his job analysis revealed that principals were spending 85 percent of their time on managerial tasks. He recommended that at least 45 percent of their time be spent in the classroom and even provided a daily schedule for the principal to follow that would allow for this new distribution (Cubberly, 1923, p. 46). It's interesting to note that Cubberley uses the job analysis model that had been developed during World War I.

While Ellwood P. Cubberley occupied the center ring from 1915 to 1934, other textbook writers were performing their acts. Just as Cubberley's *Public School Administration* and *The Principal and His School* played to the needs of the city, a separate and parallel literature grew up for the smaller communities and rural areas.

In 1912 Mabel Carney of Teachers College wrote *Country Life and the Country School,* which was published by Row and Peterson. This book, and others that followed in its wake, were tied to a broader national movement of concern for rural America in the age of industrialization and urbanization. Carney's book began what was to become a rather steady stream of books on rural education by authors such as J. B. Arp, C. H. Betts, and others. Seeing this area develop, the Macmillan Company asked Mabel Carney to serve as general editor of its Rural Education Series. Two of these books, *Rural School Management* by Ina Barnes in 1929 and *Principles of Rural School Administration* by Julian Butterworth in 1926, directly concern administration. Butterworth held the title of Professor of Rural Education at Cornell University, which was very active in the rural movement. The majority of Butterworth's quotations come from bulletins of the U.S. commissioner of education and the 1922 Survey of Rural Education in the state of New York, undertaken by Carney, Judd, Butterworth, and others. Barnes was a rural school supervisor in LaGrange County, Indiana. Her use of the word "management" is really intended as classroom management vis-à-vis William Chandler Bagley, rather than being concerned with administration. Several of the large publishers either began series or encouraged textbooks dealing with rural education at this time, and Houghton Mifflin was among them. Thus, Cubberley was again at the forefront.

Cubberley's *Rural Life and Education* was published in 1914, before he turned his attention to city schools. Even after moving into urban education, however, Cubberley kept his fingers on the pulse of the rural education movement. In 1925 John Almack and James Bursch wrote *The Administration of Consolidated and Village Schools* for the Riverside Series.

James F. Bursch was an assistant professor at the Oregon Agricultural College, but coauthor John C. Almack was an associate professor at Stanford under Dean Cubberley. It's interesting to note that by the 1930s most of the regional efforts at textbook writing had disappeared. Undoubtedly, part of this is attributable to the phasing out of small book printers and the consolidation of commercial houses, coupled with more national approaches to school problems. One book that disproves the rule, however, is R. V. Hunkins's *The Superintendent at Work in Smaller Schools*, published by D. C. Heath in 1931. Hunkins was superintendent in Leadville, South Dakota. There are no footnotes where one might trace Hunkins's sources, but at the end of his book, he mentions five books of extreme importance—one is the Almack and Bursch book previously mentioned; another is Ward Reeder's *The Fundamentals of Public School Administration,* and the last three are all titles written by Cubberley.

The various titles that concerned themselves with rural school administration utilized many of the generalizations that were emerging from sociology. This was also true of those texts that concerned urban education. The difference seems to be that the rural books were using social analytic frameworks, while the urban-related books were using job and bureaucratic analyses. It really wasn't popular for urban books to use social analysis until the 1960s.

I have intended to show that Cubberley dominated the books on city school administration prior to 1933, but it would be wrong to suggest that he had a monopoly. George D. Strayer and N. L. Engelhardt's *Problems in Educational Administration* was published by Teacher College's Bureau of Publications in 1925. Carter Alexander, Paul Mort, and others contributed to this 750-page volume. Although it incorporates an excellent bibliography, some of the latest work done at Teacher's College (such as the Strayer-Haig financial formulas), and a thorough coverage of a number of vital topics, it doesn't really compete with Cubberley's work since it was not published by a commercial house. Another example of an administrative text published before 1933 would be Oscar Weber's *Problems in Public School Administration,* published by Century in 1930.

From the 1920s onward, it should be noted that a group of administrative subspecialties come into full bloom. I have previously alluded to school law. In addition to law, finance and supervision of curriculum and instruction come into being. Selecting finance as an example shows books such as Strayer and Haig's *Financing of Education in the State of New York,* Pittenger's *An Introduction to Public School Finance,* Moehlman's *Public School Finance,* Engelhardt's *Public School Business Administration,* and Reeder's *The Business Administration of a School System* all being published between 1923 and 1929.

Cubberley's near monopoly of general school-administrative texts continued with his publication of *State School Administration: A Textbook of Principles* in 1927. The format was typical of his earlier works. Roughly the first third of the book is devoted to historical evolution, and the latter two-thirds deals with problems. Throughout his long period of productivity, Cubberley favored strong state systems of education as best confronting the double-edged sword of localism and federal control. The state promised to be the best vehicle for supervising local school districts.

In 1933 Ellwood P. Cubberley retired from Stanford. He left the field of publishing having witnessed the rise of the textbook as a primary tool in the training of school administrators. This primacy would continue into subsequent epochs.

REFERENCES

Almack, John C., and Bursch, James F. (1925). *The administration of consolidation and village schools.* Boston: Houghton Mifflin.

Ayer, Fred C., and Barr, A. S. (1928). *The organization of supervision.* New York: Appleton.

Barnes, Ina G. (1929). *Rural school management.* New York: Macmillan.

Butterworth, Julian. (1926). *Principles of rural school administration.* New York: Macmillan.

Callahan, Raymond. (1962). *Education and the cult of efficiency.* Chicago: University of Chicago Press.

Carney, Mabel. (1912). *Country life and the country school.* Chicago: Row and Peterson.

Chancellor, William E. (1904). *Our schools: their administration and supervision.* Boston: Heath.

Cubberley, Elwood P. (1923). *The principal and his school: the organization, administration, and supervision of instruction in an elementary school.* Boston: Houghton Mifflin.

Cubberley, Ellwood P. (1916). *Public school administration.* Boston: Houghton Mifflin.

Cubberley, Ellwood P. (1905). *School funds and their apportionment.* New York: Teachers College Contributions to Education.

Cubberley, Ellwood P. (1914). *School and county education reorganization: the revised constitution and school code of the State of Osceola.* New York: Macmillan.

Cubberley, Ellwood P. (1927). *State school administration: a textbook of principles.* Boston: Houghton Mifflin.

Cubberley, Ellwood P. (1904). *Syllabus of lectures on the history of education: with selected bibliographies and suggestions as to reading.* New York: Macmillan.

Cubberley, Ellwood P., and Edward Elliott. (1915). *State and county school administration.* Vol. 2. New York: Macmillan.

Culter, Horace M., and Stone, Julia M. (1913). *The rural school: Its methods and management.* New York: Silver Burdett.

Dutton, Samuel T. (1903). *School management: practical suggestions concerning the conduct and life of the school.* New York: Scribner's.

Dutton, Samuel T., and Snedden, David. (1909). *The administration of public education in the United States.* New York: Macmillan.

Hanus, Paul. (1920). *School administration and school reports.* Boston: Houghton Mifflin.

Hanus, Paul. (1913). *School efficiency: a constructive study applied to New York City.* Yonkers: World Book Co.

Hines, L. N. (1911). The ideal school board from the superintendent's point of view. *Proceedings of the National Education Association* 7 (January, 1894): 994–1002.

Hinsdale, R. A. (1894). The American school superintendent. *Educational Review* 7 (January): 42–54.

Hunkins, R. V. (1931). *The superintendent in work in smaller schools.* Boston: Heath.

Koos, Leonard V. (1917). *The administration of secondary school units.* Vol. 7. Supplementary Educational Monographs. Chicago: University of Chicago Press, p. 13.

Maxwell, William H. (1912). *A quarter century of public school development.* New York: American Book Co.

Monroe, Paul (ed.). (1911). *A cyclopaedia of education.* New York: Macmillan.

Sears, Jesse B. (1925). *The school survey: a textbook on the use of school surveying in the administration of public schools.* Boston: Houghton Mifflin.

Sears, Jesse B., and Henderson, Adin D. (1957). *Cubberley of Stanford.* Stanford: Stanford University Press.

Strayer, George D., and Engelhardt, N. L. (1925). *Problems in education administration.* New York: Teachers College, Columbia University.

Strayer, George D., and Thorndike, Edward L. (1913). *Educational administration: quantitative studies.* New York: Macmillan.

Suzzallo, Henry. (1906). *The rise of local school supervision in Massachusetts.* New York: Teachers College, Columbia University.

Weber, Oscar F. (1930). *Problems in public school administration.* New York: Century.

4

From Conventional Wisdom to Concept: School-Administration Texts, 1934–1945

James C. Parker

Educational-administration textbook writers during the period from 1934 to 1945 sought to interpret and apply two opposing educational philosophies: the school as the agency of society and the school as the pioneer of society (Newsom and Langfitt, 1940, p. 1). Partly in reaction to the unquestioning scientism of the then conventional school-administration wisdom and partly in reaction to the economic and social upheaval of the Great Depression, the writers struggled to formulate a new conception of school administration based on cooperation, participation, and democracy. But they were reluctant to denigrate conventional wisdom. Thus, with two exceptions, the textbooks reviewed for this chapter present a dualism characteristic of the period: distilled conventional wisdom and fermenting concept. Newlon, the analytic philosopher, and Koopman, Miel, and Misner, the practitioner engineers, are the exceptions. Throughout their books they advocate and demonstrate the emerging concepts of cooperation, participation, and democracy.

The writers of the textbooks reviewed in detail were overwhelmingly men and professors of education or secondary education. Only one, Alice Miel, an instructor at Teachers College, was female, and only one, Dennis Cooke of George Peabody College for Teachers, was designated in his book at the time of publication a professor of administration.

In an attempt to depict and characterize this period as revealed through school-administration textbooks, answers to the following questions will be attempted. What influences and problems inherited from previous years continued during the 1930s and 1940s? How did the literature of the period define and describe school administration? And, what were the purposes and functions of school administration?

This chapter will discuss specific topics and how they are treated in the literature examined. The following textbooks will be reviewed in detail in the course of the discussion:

Phillip L. Cox and R. Emerson Langfitt. (1934). *High School Administration and Supervision*.

Jesse H. Newlon. (1934). *Educational Administration As Social Policy*.

James H. Dougherty, Frank A. Gorman, and Claude A. Phillips. (1936). *Elementary School Organization and Management*.

Samuel L. Weber. (1937). *Cooperative Administration and Supervision of the Teaching Personnel*.

Dennis H. Cooke. (1939). *Administering the Teaching Personnel*.

William N. Newsom and Emerson R. Langfitt. (1940). *Administrative Practices in Large High Schools*.

Leonard V. Koos et al. (1940). *Administering the Secondary School*.

Julian E. Butterworth and Virgil Ruegsegger. (1941). *Administering Pupil Transportation*.

Vernon H. Culp. (1942). *How to Manage a Rural School*.

Robert G. Koopman, Alice Miel, and Paul Misner. (1943). *Democracy in School Administration*.

Frederick A. Ford. (1958). *The Instructional Program: Its Organization and Administration*.

TEACHER PREPARATION

Although much progress had been made in the preparation of teachers during the previous quarter-century, lack of preparation for teaching continued to concern school-administration textbook writers. Many elementary and secondary schools, rural and urban, continued to be "filled with raw recruits drawn from the upper elementary and high school grades, with meager academic equipment and with little or no previous pedagogic guidance" (Weber, 1937, p. 17). Data from the National Survey of the Education of Teachers, commissioned by Congress and published in 1933, tends to support this notion of unpreparedness. The national survey showed that 26 percent of all teachers nationally had one year or less of college. Forty-six percent had two years of college, 16 percent had three years, and 10 percent had four years. About 2 percent had one or more years of graduate work (Weber, 1937, p. 64). Teachers with the least amount of preparation were usually found in small, rural schools, while those with the most preparation were usually found in the cities. Supervision, in-service training, and the demonstration lesson were not luxuries. They were necessities (Cooke, 1939, p. 304). The standard was two years of preparation to teach elementary school, three years for junior high, and four years for high school (Weber, 1937, p. 65).

Since the national survey also showed there were more than enough "technically certified people" to fill all existing vacancies, writers urged that preparation and certification standards be raised not only to establish a profession of teaching comparable to law, medicine, and engineering, but also to prevent people from coming into teaching because they cannot find employment in their chosen occupations.

TEACHER-TRAINING INSTITUTIONS

In the 1930s the two-year normal schools, some of which had originally been secondary schools, were rapidly transforming themselves into teachers colleges, requiring generally the completion of a four-year high school program for admission and a four-year college program for graduation. This was seen by Samuel E. Weber, Pittsburgh Associate Superintendent in Charge of Personnel, Pittsburgh, to herald "the dawn of a teaching profession in the United States" (Weber, 1937, p. 17). So encouraged was he by the teachers colleges' exaction of higher admission and graduation standards, as well as by the competition for jobs caused by teacher oversupply, that he predicted that by the 1950s the untrained and incompetent would be largely eliminated.

Certification agencies and regional accrediting associations relied heavily on teacher-training institutions to enforce established standards in terms of degrees, hours, credits, and courses and thereby to determine who would become eligible to teach. Teacher training institutions were implored to analyze carefully the positions for which they were offering training so they would not graduate or surely not certify anyone poorly qualified to hold a teaching position. One writer warned:

> The alternative point of view is for the teacher-training institution to regard itself as a kind of factory, turning out a product which meets only the coarse legal specifications, hustling for orders, and placing teachers on the basis of competition with other training agencies. Such an outlook is too much one of responsibility to the teacher candidate rather than to the pupils who are to be taught. (Koos, Hughes, Hudson, and Reavis, 1940, p. 330)

TEACHER CERTIFICATION

Originally a local school district function, the certification of teachers gradually became a state function. The trend during the period under consideration was definitely toward abolition of local certificates and centralization of certification authority in the hands of state superintendents of instruction (Koos et al., 1940, p. 327; Cooke, 1939, pp. 121–122). Also, because accrediting and certification standards were being defined in academic and professional coursework terms, teacher certification based on scholastic attainment at and credentials from recognized institutions began to supersede local and state written examinations.

As state superintendents took over the certifying function, there was a general reduction in types of certificates issued (Weber, 1937, pp. 127–129). The state office in its "detachment from those personal, pecuniary, and political influences which must always surround the actual employing situation" was a logical place to bring a degree of standardization to teacher certification, thereby making credentials valid over a wider area. Another effect of state certification was to limit the field of applicants and to indicate certain minimum attainments and qualifications (Koos et al., 1940, p. 327).

Although there was considerable variation among the states concerning certification standards, Koos et al. wrote in 1940 that there were certain recognized requirements for high school teachers. For instance, by the 1940s most states had made graduation from a four-year undergraduate program a requirement for permanent certification. However, for most states, teaching experience and a normal school certificate were still acceptable for a lower-level teaching credential. Most of the time these certificate levels also carried a salary differential, with the four-year degree carrying an increased salary (Koos et al., 1940).

Also, the types of courses required of teachers in the 1940s shifted decidedly toward required professional education courses. The number varied, depending on whether elementary or secondary certification was involved. The elementary certificates usually required about twenty-four hours in professional courses; secondary certification required perhaps as few as six semester hours (Koos et al., 1940).

Probably the most important development of this period was the development of special certificates or endorsements for specialty areas such as special education, vocations, art, music, home economics, agriculture, and business. This trend first developed in the urban schools in the 1930s and spread downward into smaller school districts.

TEACHER SALARIES AND LOAD

Teachers' salaries have historically lagged behind income levels of other professions requiring like amounts of preparation. Just prior to the Great Depression, because teachers' salaries were so low and because there were few candidates from which to choose, boards of education had "doubled teachers' salaries. Most of this increase came during the period 1919–1922" (Koos et al., 1940, p. 415). Teachers' salaries reached their highest levels in 1930–1931. But prolonged economic depression forced widespread salary reductions so that by 1934–1935, the average teacher's salary was only about 85 percent of the 1930–1931 level. By 1938–1939 salaries had regained two-thirds of the ground lost (Koos et al., 1940). Salaries did not fully recover ground lost until after World War II (Tiedeman, 1956, p. vii).

Besides the devastating effects of the Depression, two other factors, according to Weber (1937), contributed during the 1930s and the early 1940s to a precarious salary situation:

1. The overproduction of teacher supply by competing state-supported institutions and by private higher institutions offering like courses
2. The district system (ward boards) of school administration, which

readily lends itself to a devastating competition, preventing the rais-
ing of both standards and wages (p. 173)

Weber recommended in his textbook an Annapolis- or West Point–like
selection system to choose people to be trained as teachers and, thus, to
remedy the problems cited. But such was not to be the case.

Salaries in 1930–1931, the year they were the highest, ranged from a
median low in small towns (population: 2,500–5,000) of $1,200 per year
for junior high school teachers to a median high in the largest cities (population: 100,000 +) of $2,800 for senior high school teachers. (The range
for the median low $1,200 figure was $700–$1,900 per year.) By 1938–
1939 comparable median salary figures were $1,283 for junior high teach-
ers and $2,672 for senior high teachers. In the recovery process, junior
high teachers obviously fared better than senior high teachers. Elementary
teachers' salaries were below those of their secondary school counterparts
and in 1938–1939 ranged from a median low in small towns of $1,096
per year to a median high of $2,217 in the largest cities (Koos et al., 1940,
pp. 418–419). In 1940 the average salary for all teachers was $1,325 per
year (Butts, 1955, p. 543).

Although teachers' salaries and other public employees' salaries did
not drop percentagewise as drastically as those of lawyers, physicians and
surgeons, and dentists in the private sector, these private-sector salaries
never reached the absolute low levels of teachers' salaries (Cooke, 1939,
p. 284). Koos et al., commenting on teachers' salaries during the worst
of the Depression, said teachers' salaries were miniscule, but nonetheless
remained fairly stable at least for the first years of the Depression. And,
they continued to say that then, as today, other professions (largely popu-
lated by men rather than women) were more attractive in terms of financial rewards and social status. Many of these professional positions, of
course, required approximately the same amount of training and experience (Koos et al., p. 418).

They argued for a cost-of-living factor in any salary schedule and observed that the prevailing salaries for teachers assumed celibacy and no
dependents; this, they said, caused teaching to be a "profession" (Koos et
al., 1940, pp. 429–430).

Generally, the textbook writers argued for a single salary schedule for
both elementary and secondary teachers. They deplored the "Blue Law"

prohibitions of some teachers' contracts and the practice of some school districts in not hiring married women or in terminating women teachers when they did marry (Cooke, 1939, pp. 70–72, 136). Because the teaching profession was overwhelmingly female, the textbook writers, urging the correction of imbalance, advocated that men's salaries remain higher than women's—a common practice at the time (Koos et al., 1940, pp. 346, 420–422). The 1933 National Survey of the Education of Teachers showed that 75.8 percent of junior high teachers were female and 65.1 percent of senior high teachers were female (Koos et al., 1940, p. 346). Butts (1955) reported that in 1934, 80 percent of all teachers were female (p. 544). The writers searched for a salary schedule formula by which to raise salaries; but lacking any real authority to raise monies, they had to settle for explicating the principles of salary administration. The principles stated usually included the following: prepare a definite compensation plan, research average practice in surrounding communities, include a cost-of-living factor for your specific community, consider the grade level taught, consider the amount of training possessed, recognize the length of experience, consider the individual's competency, and do not ignore the criterion of supply and demand (Koos et al., 1940, pp. 423–441).

As in the case of salary, textbook writers sought a formula by which to measure teachers' loads. One often repeated device was the relative weighting of one subject area against other areas. Several writers cited a table of the relative weights of subjects as devised by Lyon County (Kansas) high school teachers (Cooke, 1939, p. 253; Weber, 1937, pp. 339–447).

In junior highs and senior highs, typical classes were all larger in 1935–1936 than in 1930–1931. Only in kindergarten classes were enrollments smaller, reflecting a population decrease spurred by the Depression (Cooke, 1939, pp. 240–241). The writers made suggestions—eliminate small high schools, departmentalize grades 7 through 12, assign teachers to subject areas vertically, rather than horizontally by grades, and limit the number of subjects which a teacher is certified to teach. But not until schools could be better financed and the population decline could work its way upward through the grades was there to be much change (Koos et al., 1940, pp. 406–412).

These teacher problems were not new, but they continued to occupy much space in school-administration textbooks. And there were other problems as well. One of these concerned the small school and related to teacher preparation, salary, and load problems already mentioned.

SMALL AND RURAL ELEMENTARY SCHOOLS

There continued to be in the 1930s and 1940s textbook writers who addressed the work of the teacher-administrator. *Elementary School Organization and Management* by Dougherty, Gorman, and Phillips (1936) and *How to Manage a Rural School* (1942) by Culp are examples of books that continue to address a hundred-year-old school-administration problem. Both of these books obviously met an accepting audience, for Dougherty, Gorman, and Phillips published a revised edition in 1950, and Culp's book went into its seventh printing in 1947. These books addressed problems of the small elementary school and its teacher.

Dougherty, Gorman, and Phillips wrote: "While the book is *specifically* designed to be used in connection with the training and practices of the *classroom teachers,* yet the elementary school principal and probably the supervisor may find it useful" (Dougherty, Gorman and Phillips, 1936, p. vi). It was not until the 1950 revised edition that a chapter on "The Elementary School Principal" was added.

Indicating that rural classes were taught by "raw recruits," as mentioned earlier in this chapter, Culp said of his *How to Manage a Rural School*:

> This material was prepared for students in training. Much of the available material in *Rural School Management* was found to be too difficult for students who recently finished high school work. The writer has attempted to include necessary material and discard padding that was often included to make a large volume. (Culp, 1942, p. 1)

Culp in 1942 was director of rural education, Northern State Teachers College, Aberdeen, South Dakota.

The problems of the small and rural schools were (1) their teachers were less prepared and had a shorter tenure than the large and city school teachers, (2) the uppermost two elementary grades (7 and 8) were increasingly being taken over by the mushrooming secondary schools, and (3) they generally were too small and too isolated to offer a socialization program increasingly being advocated and found in progressive schools. Yet the hundreds of school boards for one- and two-teacher schools tenaciously held on to their schools.

Academic and professional preparation of rural teachers as compared with city teachers was woefully inadequate. If the same professional requirement of two to four years' training expected of city teachers were to have been adopted in rural schools, "nearly 62 percent of the rural teachers would be forcibly divorced from their jobs" (Culp, 1942, p. 9). "Yet the demands on the rural teacher for a broader, more comprehensive education to meet the needs of diverse aged students made the teacher preparation problem even more vexing" (Culp, 1942, p. 19).

Elementary schools, particularly small ones, were being reorganized from the top—by secondary schools—to meet some of their shortcomings. Since an emerging democratic philosophy called for a shift from administrative convenience to the child's interests, attitudes, and activities, secondary schools frequently reorganized grades 7 and 8 into a vertically integrated program to meet program needs that a one- or two-teacher school could not, or that a small grades 9 through 12 secondary school alone could not. Dougherty, Gorman, and Phillips commented that there was no typical elementary school pattern—elementary schools included nine or eight or seven or six years, some with kindergartens and some without them. Organization of elementary schools, they said, fell into two categories: "(1) that concerned primarily with the activities within the classroom, and (2) that concerned with activities necessary for interclassroom relationships" (Dougherty et al., 1936, p. 21). And it was in the second category that the one-room school was unable to provide the necessary socializing experiences.

Finally, school-administration textbook writers were concerned that modern means of transportation were not being utilized for improved school programs. The old one-and-a-half-mile walking distance dogma was being held too closely. Small rural schools ranged in size from two to seven pupils; the average rural school had from twelve to fifteen pupils. Combining schools and utilizing modern transportation held the possibility that a large enough pupil base could be established for a complete school program, including a socializing one (Culp, 1942, p. 9). Textbook writers wished to consolidate small schools into larger ones to overcome program isolation, but they also wished to avoid the perceived anonymity and crime of the larger community (Culp, 1942, pp. 13–17).

GROWTH OF SECONDARY EDUCATION

Whereas in 1900 only about 10 percent of the fourteen to eighteen year olds in the United States were enrolled in high schools, by 1936 approximately 65 percent to 70 percent were enrolled in high schools (Koos et al., 1940, p. 1; Cox and Langfitt, 1934, p. vii). High school or secondary education became synonymous with the people's college—in fact, since the junior college's founding in 1902 at Joliet, Illinois, many secondary schools included grades thirteen and fourteen, junior college. Junior high schools, founded about 1909–1910 in California and Ohio, also swelled secondary school enrollments (Butts, 1955, p. 540; Newsom and Langfitt, 1940, p. 5). This tremendous expansion of secondary education spurred an administrative literature focus all its own.

In the twentieth century, the American public began to value extended schooling for their children and for themselves. From approximately 6,000 public secondary schools, 20,000 secondary school teachers, and a half-million secondary school students in 1900, the numbers by 1936 had risen to almost 26,000 schools, 270,000 teachers, and 6 million students. By 1940 there were between 6.5 million and 7 million students enrolled in public secondary schools. This was nothing short of phenomenal growth (Butts, 1955, p. 542; Newsom and Langfitt, 1940, p. 6).

As secondary education grew in magnitude and importance, so did the principalship of ever-growing high schools. From an average size of 124 pupils in 1918, the high school had grown to an average of 233 in 1932, almost doubling in size (Cox and Langfitt, pp. 9–10). The median size of high schools was reported in the National Survey of Secondary Education data as 721 pupils in 1932 (Koos et al., 1940, p. 7). By 1940, Newsom and Langfitt and eight other practicing principals of secondary schools were impressed enough with the number and problems of large secondary schools that they wrote a textbook, *Administrative Practices in Large High Schools*. The ten contributing principals were at schools ranging from a 1,050-pupil, 35-teacher junior high school to a 4,000-pupil, 160-teacher senior high school.

Secondary education had grown so fast not only in numbers, organization, and scope, but also in programs and purposes that its fundamental functions were not delineated and accepted, even by school administrators and teachers. To help remedy this crisis of identity, the Committee on the Orientation of Secondary Education, Department of Secondary School Principals, National Education Association, published in 1936 the following list of controversial issues (Newsom and Langfitt, 1940, pp. 10–11):

1. Shall secondary education be provided at public expense for all normal individuals or for only a limited number?
2. Shall secondary education seek to retain all pupils in school as long as they wish to remain, or shall it transfer them to other agencies under educational supervision when, in the judgment of the school authorities, these agencies promise to serve better the pupils' immediate and probable future needs?
3. Shall secondary education be concerned only with the welfare and progress of the individual, or with these only as they promise to contribute to the welfare and progress of society?
4. Shall secondary education provide a common curriculum for all, or differentiated offerings?
5. Shall secondary education include vocational training or shall it be restricted to general education?
6. Shall secondary education be primarily directed toward preparation for advanced studies, or shall it be primarily concerned with the value of its own courses, regardless of a student's future academic career?
7. Shall secondary education accept conventional school subjects as fundamental categories under which school experiences shall be classified and presented to students, or shall it arrange and present experiences in fundamental categories directly related to the performance of such functions of secondary schools in a democracy as increasing the ability and the desire to meet sociocivic, economic, health, leisure-time, vocational, and preprofessional problems and situations?

8. Shall secondary education present merely organized knowledge, or shall it also assume responsibility for attitudes and ideals?

9. Shall secondary education seek merely the adjustment of students to prevailing social ideals, or shall it seek the reconstruction of society?

10. Granting that education is a "gradual, continuous, unitary process," shall secondary education be presented merely as a phase of such a process, or shall it be organized as a distinct but closely articulated part of the entire education program, with peculiarly emphasized functions of its own?

DIFFERENTIATION OF ADMINISTRATION

With growth in length and breadth of schooling expected by the public came growth in the numbers and types of school functionaries. School administration was increasingly divided into distinct conceptual categories, and with a growing cadre of middle managers, school administrators at various levels tried to differentiate their roles and responsibilities. This differentiation effort was especially noticeable between superintendents and principals. Mention has already been made of the growth of a special body of literature concerning secondary education.

ADMINISTRATION—CURRICULUM MAKING—SUPERVISION

Older textbooks dealt with administration, supervision, and curriculum making in one volume and as unitary or at least as closely integrated school-administration tasks. An example of a comprehensive text is Ellwood P. Cubberly's (1922) *Public School Administration*. Textbooks of the 1930s and 1940s began to treat only one or two of these functions in a single volume. This delimitation probably reflected the growing knowledge in the field of school administration, as well as the growing size of schools and school districts. To handle such growth, categories had to be established and topics addressed.

In 1934 Cox and Langfitt stated in the preface to their 674-page textbook, "This volume undertakes to deal with the administrative and supervisory functions of the high school principal and his assistants" (p. ix). But by 1940, Koos et al., in 662 pages, intended to deal only with administration, organization, and management, as opposed to supervision and curriculum making (p. 6). The effort to write a comprehensive text in school administration seemed to have been abandoned. Instead, comprehensive administrator reading lists were included in texts, and specialized textbooks were published.

Examples of the former are lists given by Koos et al. (1940) and Douglass (1945). Koos et al.'s literature list included eleven books plus twenty-seven periodicals, seven of which dealt almost exclusively with secondary education. Interestingly, Ellwood P. Cubberley and George D. Strayer were not included in the entries (Koos et al., 1940, pp. 9–12). Douglass's list of professional reading for the high school principal was divided into three parts: (1) periodicals, fifteen entries; (2) professional books, fifty-five entries in ten categories (general secondary education, high school administration, methods of teaching, tests and measurements, guidance, supervision, curriculum, activities, general school administration, psychology of secondary education); and (3) general reading, to include regular readings of at least one "high-grade, relatively reliable newspaper" (six to choose from), one periodical from each of three classes (conservative or reactionary, liberal or progressive, middle-of-the-road or neutral; ten to choose from), assorted small books and pamphlets, plus per year six or eight well-selected current books, a few books of current fiction, and two or three older books of superlative caliber, from the Bible to Sandburg's *Abraham Lincoln, The Prairie Years* (Douglass, 1945, pp. 554–568). Of course, Douglass's own six-hundred-page volume should be read. In the extensive thirty-one-page bibliography given at the end of the Douglass book, further reading is suggested. Interestingly again, Cubberley is not referenced at all (although he was cited on the relationship of principal to janitor in one chapter and was referenced in the professional reading list) and Strayer is referenced only once. These lists represent the then current professional sources and the typical topical areas of concern for the 1930s–1940s administrator.

Specialized books in school administration could also be found. Butterworth and Ruegsegger's *Administering Pupil Transportation* (1941) is an example of a specialized book. Based on Ruegsegger's dissertation, it includes a thirty-five-page scorecard for measuring the effectiveness and quality of service of buses, routes, and transportation systems (Butterworth and Ruegsegger, 1941, pp. 51–86). In other words, it shows how to provide optimum service at minimum cost (p. 89). Further examples of specialized books include Johnston's *Administering the Guidance Program* (1941), Magill's *Administering Vocational Education* (1941), Pennock's *Administration and the Rule of Law* (1941), and a series of yearbooks published by the University of Chicago Press as a result of the annual meetings of the Conference of Administrative Officers of Public and Private Schools.

Curriculum

Curricular emphases of the public school moved haltingly in this period from college preparation to life and living—citizenship, health, recreation, vocation (Koos et al., 1940, p. 2). The expanded school curriculum was not always taught in the same building under one roof, but it was offered perhaps in a specialized vocational school and in a neighboring high school. The ten critical issues identified by the Department of Secondary-School Principals illustrate the uncertainty of a curriculum expanded beyond preparation for college. Cox and Langfitt commented that adolescents preparing for vocational occupations had been recipients of the most "realistic" secondary experience. This was because labor groups and business interests had lobbied hard for inclusion of world-of-work-type courses in secondary curricula. The obvious self-interest of these groups is in evidence when we survey the significant number of manual-training-, commercial-, and science-type high schools that grew and developed in the 1930s and 1940s (Cox and Langfitt, 1934, p. 20).

Certainly the effect of so-called progressive educators could be seen. A socialization program was advocated for rural schools (Culp, 1942, pp. 67–69), an activities program was seen as a necessary part of a modern elementary school (Dougherty et al., 1942, p. 10), and the extracurriculum, including health and physical education, assumed a greater and greater portion of school time at the secondary level (Koos et al., 1940, p. 130)—all because schools were perceived to be embryonic societies, and pupils were perceived to learn through directed living. The expanded curriculum brought with it new administrative titles—curriculum coordinator, dean of girls, dean of boys, director of vocational guidance, director of citizenship, and so forth (Cox and Langfitt, 1934, p. 47). Generally, there was a movement away from strict curriculum tracks to broader, more integrated studies centered on a core of courses taken by all (Koos et al., 1940, pp. 14–17, 42–49).

Supervision

By analyzing the writings concerning supervision during this period, one can see a change from supervision as inspectorial and state mandated to supervision focusing on the improvement of teaching and cooperatively undertaken by administrator and teacher.

Although others had written advocating cooperative supervision (Weber, 1937), Ford, as late as 1938 in his book's first chapter, "The Functions of Supervision," said, following conventional wisdom:

> The point has been reached when the state must organize an educational program in keeping with the times if school systems are to render the services expected of them. Not only must it organize such a program, but it must also follow the example of big business enterprises in seeing to it that the program is efficiently carried out—hence the necessity for effective supervision. (p. 3)

To the end stated, Ford devised scorecards with ten like quotients by which to rate teachers in the following areas: environmental and biological background for effective study, the assignment, supervised study, controls of conduct, beginning motor control, inductive-deductive procedure, appreciation, the activity program, the drill procedure, the project methods, the problem-solving procedure, the review procedure, the testing-grading procedure, the technique of socialization, the lecture procedure, general principles applicable to all procedures, and personality traits. Thus, a teacher could receive 100 on personality traits and 80 on teaching appreciation, and so forth (Ford, 1938, pp. 146–206). Obviously, the writer believed "that practically every educational effort should be measured" (Ford, 1938, p. 50).

Five years later (1943) Koopman, Miel, and Misner, in their chapter "The Nature of Educational Leadership," were advocating that consultative services replace supervision and, to turn the tables completely around, that teachers should evaluate consultative services received (Koopman, Miel, and Misner, 1943, p. 55).

Koos et al. took a middle ground between the two extremes just cited (and probably nearer actual practice) when they said:

> a study of teacher-rating plans and their actual results must convince any-one that a rating card cannot be a substitute for the rater's own extended training in values and techniques in all the subjects, his possession of a modern point of view in education, common sense, an analytical mind, and a sense of justice. (Koos et al., 1940, p. 370)

Other writers such as Cooke, however, turned the traditional supervisory tables also and devised performance checklists with which to evaluate principals, superintendents, and even school board members (Cooke, 1939, pp. 208–222). Item Number 1 on the school board rating scale: Recognizes Superintendent as Head of School System, zero points for "Refuses to recognize superintendent," through forty-five points for "Often advises superintendent how to run schools," to ninety points for the school board member who "Never interferes with administrative affairs" (Cooke, 1939, p. 218).

Cooke also presented a rating scale by which pupils could evaluate teachers. Everybody could get into the act of cooperative supervision.

SUPERINTENDENT-PRINCIPAL ROLES

Growth in the number of schools (particularly secondary schools) and in the size of school districts and expansion in curricula brought increased pressures on a district's chief educational officer to seek administrative assistance. No longer could a superintendent in a city school system, for example, be the building administrator for every school in the district. Yet practice varied widely; in small villages, and there were hundreds of them, superintendents also functioned as principals, while the principals of high school districts (e.g., California union high schools, Montana county high schools, Illinois township and community high schools) were, in function, superintendents reporting directly to a board of education (Koos et al.,

1940, p. 463). Textbook writers belabored the increasing importance and responsibility of a separate office called principal, yet, as was shown, there were few unique responsibilities attached to the office. Therefore, the following discussion in this chapter will treat the principalship and superintendency as unitary in academic and professional qualifications, certification, duties, and salary, unless distinct differentiation was made in the textbooks reviewed.

ACADEMIC AND PROFESSIONAL QUALIFICATIONS

In 1934 it was reported that generally school administrators held bachelor's degrees. A few states (California, Maryland, and New York were given as leaders) required the master's degree to qualify for administrative positions (Cox and Langfitt, 1934, p. 50). Whereas in 1930–1931 approximately 4.7 percent of secondary administrators had no degree, 47 percent had a bachelor's, 46 percent had a master's, and 2.2 percent had a doctorate, by 1940–1941, 1.8 percent had no degree, 23.3 percent had a bachelor's, 70.4 percent had a master's, and 4.5 percent had a doctorate (Douglass, 1945, p. 546). School administrators were obviously rapidly attaining advanced schooling, and a trend toward the master's degree as a minimum was obvious.

The academic training received by school administrators was a typical liberal arts degree program with "the gaps in training which seem unavoidable with the present elective system." Professionally, school administrators generally lacked training in the newer curricular fields, such as vocational subjects, music, art, and physical education (Koos et al., 1940, p. 454).

Nevertheless, professional progress was being made as degree attainment rose. Douglass, at the close of the period under consideration, was optimistic:

> It seems most probable that the high-school principalship of the near future, along with the school superintendency, will require not only distinctly superior mental and personal characteristics but continued technical and professional training, and affording responsibility and prestige on a par with that

of the more generally recognized professions of medicine, law, and architecture. (Douglass, 1945, p. 546)

CERTIFICATION

With rising academic and professional attainments came rising certification requirements. Regional accrediting associations and state universities that accredited high school programs certainly played a significant role in promoting and upholding certification minimums. In 1905 only one state had a special administrative credential, one for superintendent (Tyack and Cummings, 1977, p. 59). By 1923, seven states distinguished between teacher and administrator certificates, and by 1934, twenty-seven states had separate teacher and administrator certificates (Koos et al., 1940, p. 457). The requirements for administrative certification in 1934 were typically college or normal school graduation, and one to five years' experience; over half of the states required twenty semester hours of professional courses (school administration and supervision being the most frequent), and twelve states specified that the professional courses must be graduate school work (Koos et al., 1940).

DUTIES

It was in administrative duties that differentiation, although small, between superintendents and principals was reported in the textbooks. Interestingly, two textbooks reported studies that showed that the overwhelming majority of both superintendents and principals were continuing to teach in addition to performing their administrative duties (Cooke, 1939, p. 246; Koos et al., 1940, p. 464). And it was the administrative duty of appointing or nominating teachers that seemed to be most vexing for superintendents and principals. Sometimes local school board politics prevented either the superintendent's or the principal's selecting teachers (Cooke, 1939, pp. 28, 57–58; Weber, 1937, p. 187). Since superintendents had been longer in the business of selecting teachers, they evidently did not relinquish that duty readily when they actually held it. Elementary and secondary school-administration textbook writers argued for the school principal's having at least advisory authority in the selection of school personnel, for the principal has "intimate acquaintance with the positions to be filled" (Koos et al., 1940, p. 357; Dougherty et al., 1936, p. 341).

Realistically, the superintendent and the school board granted administrative power to the principal; in effect, the superintendent controlled the duties of the principalship (Cox and Langfitt, 1934, p. 47). Thus, the superintendent could make of a principalship anything from its being a clerical position to its having carte blanche concerning the educative influences of a school. The critical administrative problem was "to give the principal real professional responsibility and yet not so much independence as to endanger articulation with elementary and specialized schools" (Koos et al., p. 463). It seemed clear that a principal should approach the school board through or with the superintendent (Douglass, 1945, p. 588).

In practice the superintendency and principalship, where they were separate offices, were ill defined. Ayer's extensive study reported by Koos et al. attempted by means of "A Checking List of 1,000 Duties of School Administrators" to differentiate which office, superintendent or principal, performed certain duties. In the nine categories of administrative duties in Ayer's study [(1) 101 general control duties, (2) 169 executive-management duties, (3) 153 business-management duties, (4) 86 teaching-staff duties, (5) 120 pupil duties, (6) 70 curriculum duties, (7) 79 special-activities duties, (8) 106 instruction duties, and (9) 166 special-services duties], it was found that principals were performing 85 percent of the same duties as superintendents. The only category in which there appeared much variation was business management, where principals performed only two-thirds as many duties as superintendents (Koos et al., 1940, p. 464). Cox and Langfitt tended to confirm this differentiation, for they report in the preface to their textbook that "building programs and educational finance are essentially the responsibilities of school superintendents and not of principals" (Cox and Langfitt, 1934, p. x) In sum, then, except for business management and closely related duties, superintendents and principals were by and large performing the same types of functions, creating overlapping areas of responsibility and possible sources of conflict.

SALARY

Remembering that superintendents were often supervising principals in practice and vice versa, one can assume the principal's and the superintendent's salaries were the same in many cases. Data was reported for 1930–1931 (the year salaries were generally the highest for teachers and administrators), 1938–1939, and 1942–1943 (see table 4–1). Using elementary teachers' salary (1930–1931) as a base of 100, principals' (junior and senior high included) salaries ranged from 50 percent to 150 percent above the base (Koos et al., 1940, p. 445). The wider range of salaries at the junior high administrative level was likely the result of a higher percentage of principals at that level in the smaller communities being women, whereas men were more likely to be principals in larger communities and to be paid more (Koos et al., 1940, p. 422). The writers thought administrative salaries were competitive with, though certainly not as high as, other professions and businesses requiring like amounts of ability, training, and experience (Koos et al., 1940, p. 445).

Douglass also reported superintendents' salaries for 1942–1943. They ranged from $359 per year in the smallest villages (population 2,500–5,000) to $8,542 per year in the largest cities (population 100,000+). Where there were superintendents separate and apart from principals in the smallest villages, superintendents were likely to earn approximately half again as much as the high school principals, but in the largest cities, superintendents were likely to earn almost three-quarters again as much.

Table 4-1   Median Yearly Salaries for Junior High and Senior High School Principals by Smallest (Pop. 2,500–5,000) and Largest (Pop. 100.000+) Cities.

Year	Position	*Salary:* $2,500–5,000	$100,000+	*Relationship: Small to Large Population (% increase)*
1930–1931[1]	Junior high principal	1,775	4,500	150
	Senior high principal	2,403	5,100	112
1938–1939[1]	Junior high principal	1,579	4,359	176
	Senior high principal	2,156	4,758	121
1942–1943[2]	Junior high principal	1,757	4,422	152
	Senior high principal	2,317	4,913	112

1. Compiled from Koos et al., 1940, p. 422.
2. Compiled from Douglass, 1945, p. 550.

For both the principalship and the superintendency, the more lucrative positions in the 1930s and 1940s were in the big cities. It is informative to note also that administrative salaries had not by 1942–1943, the beginning of World War II, reached the levels of 1930–1931.

Finally, there had to be some less formal survival relationships between a principal and the school district's central office. A glimpse into those relationships was given when Cox and Langfitt suggested that a principal's fiat was law unless and until the principal was overruled by the superintendent or the community (Cox and Langfitt, 1934, p. 53). It was also suggested that the principal was viewed as the "protector" of teachers from a central office supervisor who could snuff out originality and initiative in the classroom (Cox and Langfitt, 1934, p. 664). And at the end of a long book (674 pages), Cox and Langfitt gave the beginning principal two pieces of survival advice: your "conduct must conform to the standards set by influential conservative citizens" (Cox and Langfitt, 1934, p. 669), and on the next to the last page of the text, "there is a very high correlation between the administrative competency of a principal and his personal solvency" (Cox and Langfitt, 1934, p. 673).

SOCIETAL REFORM AND SCHOOL ADMINISTRATION

What was happening in American society surrounding the Depression and what was happening in the world during the 1930s and 1940s surrounding the development of totalitarian versus democratic states could not be ignored. But it was not just these events that caused men—such as John Dewey, Boyd H. Bode, William H. Kilpatrick, and George S. Counts—to advance new conceptions of the purpose of education and subsequently of the purpose of school administration. The crux of the matter was whether schools were to be "the agency of society and as such should provide those experiences which will develop in youth the ideals, habits, and skills necessary to enable him to take his place in that society" or whether schools were to be "the pioneer of society and as such must assume a major share of responsibility for the development of a society which will provide the greatest good for all and produce individuals who are willing to work toward such an end" (Newsom and Langfitt, 1940, p. 1).

REFORMULATION OF THE
PURPOSES OF EDUCATION

School-administration textbook writer Jesse H. Newlon gave a clarion call
to reformulate the purposes of education as well as school administration.
His book *Educational Administration As Social Policy* (1934), a volume
in the American Historical Association's Investigation of the Social Studies in the Schools, was seminal to the development of the profession and
represents, even today, against the backdrop of administrative efficiency
experts, a pertinent rethinking of the field. Other textbook writers followed the lead of Newlon, but he was among the first, if not the very first,
in administration to question sharply the then conventional wisdom.

Writing under the heading "The Social Purposes of National Systems
of Education," Newlon stated that education in the United States had four
basic purposes: (1) transmission of the culture, (2) education for citizenship, (3) social control, and (4) vocational efficiency (Newlon, 1934, pp.
54–58). In its attempt to accomplish these purposes, "the American
school has, in large measure, been conducted as though it were educating
individuals for a static society. A few have discerned the significance of
the rapid social changes of the nineteenth and twentieth centuries" (p. 64).
Even the scientific method, which had succeeded in eliminating some ob-
solete materials and adding other new items to the school curriculum, had
failed to be concerned with the basic social and educational purposes of
schools and had not questioned the established order of things (p. 65). The
essence of Newlon's criticism was that the American system of education
has largely reflected laissez-faire individualism; that the scientific method
in education, while making a desirable contribution, has at the same time
tended to crystallize traditional educational procedures; that although a
critical school of thought has arisen that would bring education more
closely into contact with life and give it definite social direction, American education as a whole has, as yet, been but little affected by this new
movement that would fashion American education not only around "the
corporate character of modern life," but also around "an extension of the
principle of democracy in the direction of planning our industrial and economic life under collective control" (Newlon, 1934, p. 69). These were
bold words, obviously reflecting the thinking of progressive educators.

Ten years later the words would not seem so bold as other school-administration textbook writers joined Newlon in a call for reformulating the purpose of schooling. Dougherty, Gorman, and Phillips (1936) proclaimed that democratic socialization should be the unitary objective of education (p. 43). Koopman, Miel, and Misner (1943) observed, "In a present-day totalitarian state the individual is taught to cooperate with the state according to an authoritarian political theory. In a present-day democratic state the individual learns to cooperate with the state and with other individuals according to a democratic political theory" (p. 20). With a reformulation of the purposes of education, a reconceptualization of school administration was in order.

DEMOCRATIC ADMINISTRATION

In school-administration textbooks, writers during the early years of the period began rather subtly and unobtrusively to suggest that teachers and administrators should cooperate in improving teaching through the supervisory process and that the day of the autocratic administrator should be past (Weber, 1937, pp. 327–328). By 1939 Cooke, sensing a change, entitled the first chapter of his book "Considering Teachers As Human Beings" and reported that business and industry had already discovered the salutary effects of attention to workers and their morale (pp. 1, 8). He viewed teacher participation in administration as "an effective means of educating teachers in service" (p. 318). Evidently, professors of school administration in Missouri did not necessarily agree, for of teachers, superintendents and principals, and professors of school administration surveyed, the professors were the most conservative in their view of how much teachers should participate in administrative functions (Cooke, 1939, p. 322).

Generally, school-administration textbook writers after 1940 portrayed teachers as the relative equals of administrators, as necessary to the execution of administrative policy, and as valuable contributors to cooperative procedures, which, they said, produced better plans and programs than one person alone could. Because of these factors, "teachers should share in the exercise of administrative control over the schools" and "democracy should prevail in school administration" (Koos et al., 1940, pp. 481–482). Teacher participation meant democratic administration.

Koopman, Miel, and Misner (1943) in their *Democracy in School Administration* attempted to "translate democracy into action," in other words, to offer a practice-oriented, how-to approach to extant democratic administration philosophy and theory (p. v). Getting the foundation of their beliefs up front, they used an excerpted version of Dewey's "Democracy for the Teacher" as the textbook's frontispiece (pp. xiii–xiv). According to the writers, "Group policymaking is an essential element in democratic administration" (p. 50). To this end, a policy-making individual school as well as a citywide committee system for enfranchising teachers in their democratic administration roles and responsibilities was proposed (pp. 76–121). The writers' administrative credo was summarized in twelve "imperative considerations" (p. 322):

1. The substitution of group control for individual control
2. The implementation of purposes through appropriate internal organization
3. The utilization of group reactions in administration of education
4. The facing of social studies
5. The building of an organization broad enough to guarantee flexibility
6. The building of an organization functional enough to protect the teacher's energies
7. Provision for the needs of all groups simultaneously
8. Continuous appraisal as a guarantee of progress
9. Cooperation as a residue of a great variety of group activities
10. Participation as an aid to learning
11. Community improvement through a dynamic functional curriculum
12. The abolition of administrative vetoes, reservations, and sacred prerogatives

But there was not unanimous agreement that group procedures, teacher participation, and democratic administration would necessarily improve schools, teaching, or administration unless

the school is benefited by (1) his own growth to greater effectiveness, and (2) his improving the administration of rules, practices, or curriculum as the result of a greater understanding of them; and unless it can be shown that the advantages are greater than the disadvantages, such as consumption of staff time, slowing down of actions or decisions or maladministration to some degree or in some instances. (Douglass, 1945, p. 573)

Democratic administration had been proposed and an attempt at engineering it into action had been given. According to one estimate, however, democratic administration was actually practiced in half the secondary schools to at least some extent (Douglass, p. 322).

PRACTICE-THEORY DUALISM

Despite the reformulation of the purposes of education and the conceptualization of new functions of school administration, average practices—some like Newlon would probably say the conventional wisdom in new clothes—continued to influence heavily the formulation and practice of school administration. The scientific movement in education, the efficiency movement in school administration, and the school survey technique in public schools all tended methodologically to emphasize central tendency and average practice.

Typically, textbooks of this period would have chapters on buildings and grounds; equipment and supplies; the layout of the principal's office; school office standards, procedures, and forms; school finance, and business administration; the selection of the staff; the organization of the curriculum; the daily schedule; personnel records; school publicity; teachers' loads; and the improvement of teaching personnel in service. Such chapters would be filled with numerous tables, lists, and charts indicating average practice in various sized communities in various parts of the country. Butterworth and Ruegsegger stated very plainly that one purpose of their textbook on transportation was the determination of prevailing standards of practice and said, "In this field, the 'ideal' is presumably that which is ahead of today's practice; the superior practice of a few systems today becomes the ideal toward which all systems are striving tomorrow" (Butterworth and Ruegsegger, 1941, p. 4).

Surveys of all kinds almost always reported average practice, and there were several nationally important and influential ones cited. Among the surveys read widely by the textbook writers were the following:

William J. Cooper and Leonard V. Koos. (1932). *National Survey of Secondary Education.*

Edward S. Evenden. (1933). *National Survey of the Education of Teachers.*

Cooperative Study of Secondary School Standards. (1938). *How to Evaluate a Secondary School.*

Walter D. Cocking and Kenneth R. Williams. (1940). *The Education of School Administrators.*

John Lund. (1941). *Education of School Administrators.*

Ten practicing principals wrote eighteen of the twenty chapters in *Administrative Practices in Large High Schools,* reporting on practices in their respective high schools. Conforming to this emphasis was the intent of Koopman, Miel, and Misner (1943) in *Democracy in School Administration* when they indicated the book was written for teachers who might want to know the experiences of practitioners in implementing democratic administration (p. v). On balance, there was a relatively great emphasis on collecting, analyzing, and reporting average practice—the conventional.

FUNCTIONS OF ADMINISTRATION

What then were the functions of school administration? There were at least two schools of thought. On the one hand, there were those who followed Newlon and indicated the functions to be as follows:

1. To examine society critically and to participate with a community and lead in the formulation of social and educational policy (Newlon, 1934, p. 234)
2. To discover leadership and enable it to flourish (Newlon, 1934, p. 234)
3. To discover the social purposes of education and to move schools and schooling effectively toward those purposes (Newlon, 1934, p. 252)

4. To promote self-expression of all school personnel toward socially desirable purposes and values (Koopman, Miel, and Misner, 1943, p. 42)
5. To organize school as a living laboratory in democratic political theory (Koopman, Miel and Misner, 1943, p. 81)
6. To cultivate an authority of reason to supplant an outmoded authority of position (Koos, Hudson, and Percival, 1940, p. 172)
7. To interpret the community to the school and the school to the community so they each can understand the other's need (Kooset et al., 1940, p. 635)

Those represented by Douglass, reluctant to relinquish the conventional wisdom, indicated the functions somewhat differently:

1. To engineer the contributions of the educational scientist into useful forms (Weber, 1937, pp. 20–21)
2. To organize and plan the work of the school as efficiently as possible (Cox and Langfitt, 1934, p. 69)
3. To supervise and lead in the improvement of teaching (Cox and Langfitt, 1934, p. 69)
4. To manage the school day to day toward identified purposes of education (Cox and Langfitt, 1934, p. 69)
5. To keep adequate records and accounts of school activities and functions (Cox and Langfitt, 1934, p. 67)
6. To protect teachers and other staff who pioneer in improving practice (Cox and Langfitt, 1934, p. 67)
7. To cooperate with the community and parents who are the stockholders and consumers of the school (Cox and Langfitt, 1934, p. 68)

By the end of the period, even the traditionalists no longer perceived schools as institutions isolated from their communities. Although the traditionalists would not agree with Newlon that the conventional forms and methods of school administration were relatively unimportant and sterile, they would agree with him that the school-administration problems of the day were largely political and social and that preparation for service should not confine itself to the mechanical, technical, and pedagogical, but rather should include a study of history, sociology, anthropology, political science, and philosophy (Newlon, 1934, pp. 252–264). School administration had almost become an applied social science.

REFERENCES

Butterworth, J. E., and Ruegsegger, V. (1941). *Administering pupil transportation*. Minneapolis: Educational Publishers.

Butts, R. F. (1955). *A cultural history of western education*. New York: McGraw-Hill.

Cocking, W. D., and Williams, K. R. (1940). *The education of school administrators*. Washington, D.C.: American Council on Education.

Cooke, D. H. (1939). *Administering the teaching personnel*. Chicago: Benjamin H. Sanborn.

Cooper, W. J., and Koos, L. V. (eds.). (1932). *National survey of secondary education* [bulletin no. 17]. Washington, D.C.: United States Office of Education.

Cooperative Study of Secondary School Standards. (1938). *How to evaluate a secondary school*. Washington, D.C.: American Council on Education.

Cox, P. W. L., and Langfitt, R. (1934). *High school administration and supervision*. New York: American Book Co.

Cubberley, E. P. (1922). *Public school administration*. Boston: Houghton Mifflin.

Culp, H. (1942). *How to manage a rural school*. Minneapolis: Burgess Publishing Co.

Dougherty, J. H., Gorman, F. A., and Phillips, C. A. (1936). *Elementary school organization and management*. New York: Macmillan.

Douglass, K. R. (1945). *Organization and administration of secondary schools*. New York: Ginn.

Evenden, E. S. (1933). *National survey of the education of teachers* [bulletin no. 10]. Washington, D.C.: United States Office of Education.

Ford, F. A. (1938). *The instructional program: its organization and administration*. New York: Prentice Hall.

Johnston, E. G. (1942). *Administering the guidance program*. Minneapolis: Educational Publishers.

Koopman, G., Miel, A., and Misner, P. J. (1943). *Democracy in school administration*. New York: Appleton-Century-Crofts.

Koos, L. V., et al. (1940). *Administering the secondary school*. New York: American Book Co.

Lund, J. (1941). *Education of school administrators* [bulletin no. 6, Federal Security Agency]. Washington, D.C.: United States Office of Education.

Magill, W. H. (1941). *Administering vocational education.* Minneapolis: Educational Publishers.

Newlon, J. H. (1934). *Educational administration as social policy.* New York: Scribner's.

Newsom, N. W., and Langfitt, R. E. (1940). *Administrative practices in large high schools.* New York: American Book Co.

Pennock, J. R. (1941). *Administration and the rule of law.* New York: Holt, Rinehart and Winston.

Tiedeman, D. V. (1956). *Teacher competence and its relation to salary.* Cambridge: New England School Development Council.

Tyack, D. B., and Cummings, R. (1977). Leadership in American public schools before 1954. In Cunningham, L., Hack, W. G., and Nystrand, R. O. (eds.), *Educational administration: the developing decades.* Berkeley: McCutchan, pp. 46–66.

Weber, S. E. (1937). *Cooperative administration and supervision of the teaching personnel.* New York: Thomas Nelson and Sons.

5

A Return to Rhetoric:
School-Administration Texts, 1946–1955

Fred D. Carver

This chapter attempts to prove the theses that (1) the dominant emphases in educational-administration textbooks in the postwar era were democratic administration and community schools, and (2) by the end of the period, a quest for a new scientific basis for administration was apparent.

The shattering experience of World War II most certainly brought the world's attention to the democratic ethic among the communities of the world. The formation of the United Nations shortly after the cessation of hostilities was intended to build world peace through a world community.

The history of educators and educational administrators had always been replete with a quasi-cult of "Americanism," democracy, and preserving the virtue of freedom in America. That texts in school administration should begin to focus on and elucidate democracy and community schools is not surprising within the context of the postwar years.

A list of textbooks published between 1946 and 1954 was developed. While certain of the volumes examined could be considered specialized (e.g., having an elementary principalship or human relations focus), excluded were texts that treated specialized task areas such as school finance (Mort and Reusser, *Public School Finance,* 1951) and subject areas such as health and physical education (Williams, Brownell, and Verbier, *The Administration of Health and Physical Education,* 1946). Also excluded were the works, whose titles identify them as exclusively treating supervision, listed here:

Harold P. Adams and Frank G. Dickey. (1953). *Basic Principles of Supervision.*

John A. Bartky. (1953). *Supervision As Human Relations.*
Charles W. Boardman et al. (1953). *Democratic Supervision in Second-ary Schools.*
Thomas H. Briggs. (1952). *Improving Instruction through Supervision.*
William T. Melchoir. (1950). *Instructional Supervision: A Guide to Modern Practice.*
Harold Spears. (1953). *Improving the Supervision of Instruction.*
Kimbal Wiles. (1950). *Supervision for Better Schools.*

The latter decision may be more questionable than the former. Supervision developed as a specialized area of administration concerned with the improvement of instruction. Almost all of the administration texts examined called attention to the improvement of instruction as the most important purpose of administration; certainly the elementary administration texts had that focus. On the surface, however, the inclusion of supervision texts in the analysis would have only added to evidence supporting the first thesis.

Finally, not included in this survey of educational-administration texts were such seminal works as Simon's *Administrative Behavior* (1947); Lepawsky's *Administration, The Art and Science of Organization and Management* (1949); and Simon, Smithburg, and Thompson's *Public Administration* (1950), used as primary source material in the early days of the behavioral science movement.

From the textbooks not excluded, a sample of nine was selected from across the nine-year period and examined with special attention paid to the preface or introduction. The following the textbooks are reviewed in detail:

Paul L. Mort. (1946). *Principles of School Administration: A Synthesis of Basic Concepts.*
Jesse B. Sears. (1947). *School Public Administration.*
Wilbur A. Yauch. (1949). *Improving Human Relations in School Administration.*
Jesse B. Sears. (1950). *The Nature of the Administrative Process.*
Benjamin R. Pittinger. (1951). *Local Public School Administration.*
Arthur B. Moehlman. (1951). *School Administration.*
John T. Wahlquist. (1952). *The Administration of Public Education.*

Edgar W. Knight. (1953). *Readings in Educational Administration.*
Douglas E. Lawson. (1953). *School Administration.*

THESIS ONE: DEMOCRATIC ADMINISTRATION
AND COMMUNITY SCHOOLS

The end of World War II is the distinct beginning of the 1946–1954 period. There was no similarly logical event in 1954 to serve as the right bookend; the *Brown vs. Board of Education* decision issued in 1954 was a milestone in the use of social/behavioral science in the framing of decisions; it would, however, be overly opportunistic to "end the period" with the decision. The year 1954 (or any specific year) is an arbitrary ending date for a period in educational-administration textbook literature that brilliantly reflects societal emphases. For all students and practitioners of educational administration during this period, the challenge was to further democratize the operation of the public schools. This had implications for internal affairs as well as external relations, since the school's democratic mission was to serve society's needs; it had to be related to and in tune with community interests and activities.

A second international conflict in the twentieth century, which involved the United States with totalitarian governments as enemies during the fighting and subsequently as allies, called to the fore the role of the public schools in preventing totalitarianism from developing and in maintaining a strong nation as protection from external forces as well. The growth of schools and school systems, in size and scope of purpose, was an additional factor calling for something other than "business as usual" in educational administration. Kefauver, introducing the design for the forty-fifth NSSE yearbook, argued the need for a reorientation of educational administration away from scientific management and suggested the use of new concepts to emphasize the difference (Henry, 1946). His new terms were educational administration as *social statesmanship, leadership in educational administration, educational planning,* and *democracy in educational administration.* Two quotes merit citing:

> The term, social statesmanship, is made appropriate, too, by the bearing that educational policy and social policy have on each other. The achievement

of important ends is dependent on the understandings, attitudes, and skills possessed by the people. In a democracy this dependence is especially critical. Likewise, educational policy has its origins in the society it serves. The school is devoted to and engaged in the service of the basic democratic principles and goals, recognizing, at the same time, its service to the individual and to the progressive improvement of society.

An important fact to be recognized, sometimes to the discomfiture of the educational administrator, is that educational policy is not a concern of the educator only. It is an appropriate and legitimate concern of people in all walks of life. (Henry, 1946, p. 3)

The concept of democracy in educational administration is now generally accepted. There are still differences of judgment as to the desirability of particular procedures, and it must be admitted that practice has not advanced as far as theory. The rise in the standard of preparation of teachers makes possible a more responsible role for the teacher. The movement is encouraged by the greater attention being paid to education for democratic citizenship and the belief that the practice of democracy is a more effective teacher than mere talk about it. (Henry, 1946, p. 3)

Only in Mort (1946), Sears (1950), and Knight (1953) was there manifest evidence of the focus on democracy as the overriding emphasis. It is not that those three books were antidemocratic. The first two were more concerned with laying out conceptualizations of administration, Mort's based on years of empirical research and Sears' based on the application of the administrative process approach from business and public administration exemplified in Gulick and Urwick's *Papers on the Science of Administration*. The third work, Knight's, was a collection of 191 short "original sources of information in educational administration." Only fourteen of the selections were authored in the 1946–1954 period. Within the administrative process focus, Sears states that the conception of education defined could "be inculcated only by teachers, principals, supervisors, and counselors who are themselves living as free individuals and working together cooperatively with mutual respect for one another, and with full consciousness of their own rights and their own duties to play a part in the government of the school" (Sears, 1950, p. 96).

In a chapter entitled "Our Theory of Public Schools," Sears (1947) asserts that principles derived from an analysis of the administrative process would be false and misleading if they are not in harmony with our theory of the state and of the public school as an instrument of the state for social control and social progress. For instance, in our form of state the concept of democracy forbids the use of authority in an autocratic way. Our organization, our controls, our directing, our planning, and our coordination must be democratic processes. (p. 109)

Yauch (1949) was writing with the elementary principal specifically in mind, but the author expressed the belief that it would be useful to administer in any role. He stated his case directly in the introductory chapter: "The present volume is an attempt to present practical suggestions concerning the ways in which the principal can provide teachers with democratic experiences" (p. 11). That theme is carried through the book in chapters such as "Group Leadership," "The Teacher's Meeting," and "The Management of Personal Relations," and the book includes specific advice/hypotheses (e.g., "Whenever any decision is made which involves others, these individuals should be included in determining the nature of that decision") (p. 208).

Pittenger (1951) comments that the democratic philosophy dominated in the published literature and at convention discussions, and that practice was being "penetrated by the movement at many points" (p. 16). In the chapter entitled "A Functional Organization of School Personnel," the dual rationale for democracy is identified as organizational efficiency and assumed inherent rights. Regarding efficiency, given a democratic institution established by a democratic society, better policies and execution will result; democracy is the necessary means for stimulating professional interest and growth, and children can learn to live in a democratic society only if that kind of environment exists for teachers.

In chapters 5 and 6, Moehlman (1959) presents principles of organization that tie together democracy, education, and administration. A later chapter is built around the theme that the democratic community and school together are the strength of American public schools. Wahlquist (1952) identified three purposes for the texts, the third (and theme of the book) being "to show how the democratic philosophy of education can be meaningfully implemented in practice" (p. iii). As an aside, the authors distinguish between school administration and educational administration. The latter, which they prefer as the field-describing term, they say, carries a dynamic connotation, while the former connotes a static area of concern, namely the school. In noting the impact of the National Conference of Professors of Educational Administration (NCPEA), the chapter author comments that NCPEA promoted democratic school administration since its inception in Endicott, N.Y., in 1947 and that "every yearbook of this body (presumably through 1950 or 1951) has been centered in this new concept" (p. 25).

The American Association of School Administrators (AASA) year-books that essentially bookend the period (1947, 1955) are replete with the democratic ideal. The administration sections of the 1947 volume, chapters 9 to 13, involve the identification of principles for the processes of democratic cooperation and then apply them in small, city, and metro-politan area school districts and at the state level. A leaning toward demo-cratic administration characterizes the 1955 volume; the yearbook was in-tended "to help people develop skills in the art of managing and working with people and maintain order and efficiency" (AASA, 1955).

The community school emphasis in the textbook literature is more im-plicit than was the emphasis on democratic administration, although Melby (1955) represents a summation of the threads that run through most of the textbooks of the period. Most had a chapter or chapters devoted to the administration of a school or relations with the community. Almost all had an introductory section that placed the school in the context of the democratic community in a democratic society. It was natural to link democratic administration with community school or, perhaps more ap-propriately, to see the community and the school as inseparable parts. In-deed, with democratic administration deriving largely from the political ideology of the society, it would have been ironic if community school or a similar concept had not emerged to remind the school of its immediate referent group.

There is some explicit evidence of the community school rhetoric in the texts as well. Sears (1947) makes the following argument in his chap-ter entitled "The Administration of a School":

Should one plan his school in ways that tend to segregate children by social groups? When the word social is properly used that is precisely what mod-ern school administration advises. This does not mean recognition of social classes. *It means that as nearly as possible a school must be for and of a real community.* [Italics added.] If the school is for a stockyards area, or an industrial section, or for a Jewish district, a Polish, Chinese, or an Italian district, or for a residential suburb, that does not in any sense mean that the pupils of any one of these groups are so segregated because they are socially below or above those of any other group. It means that each group is set off in order that the school may function in ways to fit the needs of all, adults and children, who belong to the group it serves. (p. 370)

Moehlman (1951), as previously cited, developed a chapter around the theme that the community and school together are the strength of American public schools. He also includes a section on the use of the school for adult education. The 1946 NSSE (Henry, 1946) included a chapter stressing the importance of educational administration's bringing the school and community into close working relationships. Lawson (1953) begins his text not with the general societal context setting that characterizes many of the books, but (presumably) taking all that for granted, with principles and techniques for administering school-community relations.

It may be the case that the community school concept had not yet been accepted at the level of rhetorical usage as democratic administration in the period. Or it may simply be that the community school was so much larger a concept than administration or so pregnant with curricular implications that it was on the periphery of specialized concerns for textbook writers of the period. It was a newer concept than democratic administration and could be easily subsumed for many administrators as a "given" within the societal context of the schools. As defined by Seay, it expanded the purposive parameters for the public schools and was a vehicle for the schools to act as a powerful social force within a democratic society (Henry, 1953, p. 2). It was not that the schools would "build a new social order"; it was that the schools could cooperate with communities to develop the latent capacities and improve the quality of life for all in the communities. The NSSE yearbooks toward the end of the period (Henry, 1953; Henry, 1954) no doubt gave impetus to the movement. Another, after the period ended (Henry, 1959), would rival Melby (1955) as the signal light for community education up to 1960.

THESIS TWO: A NEW QUEST

Textbooks examined revealed much less evidence that a search was beginning for a scientific basis for educational administration than that the philosophy/ideology of democratic administration dominated the period literature. Another summary judgment is that the evidence for a new quest was less pervasive than the more implicit and subtle support for the community school concept. Events of the 1946–1954 period can be chronicled that were later to crash like thunder across educational administration and to have a major impact on textbook and other literature. Hollis Moore (Griffiths, 1964, p. 11), writing of the history of educational administration, identifies 1947 as the "date to mark the beginning of a 'ferment in school administration.'" Little of the ferment found its way into the texts of the period, however.

In general, books at the end of the period differed little from those at the beginning. Immegart's descriptor of the normative educational-administration text of 1954 (presented in contrast to the typical text of 1974) would aptly describe much of the textbook literature of the period:

> The book began with an elaborate treatment of the context of education followed by a short treatment of the topic of administration. Administration in education was espoused in "democratic" terms and advanced as the way to bring democracy to organizations and the youth. Then chapters dealing with the tasks of administration were presented one by one. The book ended with a chapter or two on the challenge or future of education and re-emphasized the democratic administration charge voiced earlier for those needing reinforcement or who missed it in hurrying on to "how to do it." The context of educational administration was carefully documented with status data or survey data from secondary sources as well as the much used or respected general education literature. Research citations were largely limited to statistical studies from school districts, associations, state departments, or the United States Department of Education, and few, if any, dissertations were quoted. The case for democratic administration was less documented and once into the task areas ("how to do it") documentation was scarce while experience, successes, and opinion abounded. Included were not only guidelines, principles, and steps but also charts, forms, and procedures. And the book sought to be a complete source for the administrator (or would-be administrator), containing all he would need to or want to know in 600 or so pages. (Immegart, 1975, pp. 34–35)

Two of the textbooks stand apart as integrated and "complete conceptualizations of administration." Mort introduced *Principles of School Admin-*

istration as a "set of internally consistent principles covering the whole range of administration":

> a by-product of a search for a useful theory of educational dynamics—a theory that will put invention and the diffusion of invention of ways to meet changing concepts of purpose at the center and will modify the administrative structure and attendant procedures to meet the demands of the humanitarian and prudential principles and of empirical knowledge. (Mort, 1946)

It was not, however, a conceptualization based on the social/behavioral sciences, as were the post-1954 frameworks. It was, rather, derived largely from a practice-oriented empiricism. Sears applied a process conceptualization (organizing, controlling, directing, planning, and coordination) to "find a more fundamental basis than we now have for the criticism and improvement of administrative practice (Sears, 1947, p. viii). This work may be most important for its emphasis on the need to help people learn "how to find out how to administer" rather than training people "how to administer," and for the author's identification of psychology, sociology, anthropology, political science, law, administration (essentially public administration), and engineering and business administration as sources of subject matter to aid students (p. 501). The "helping people learn how to find out" emphasis was clearly a reaction to the how to do it/cookbook emphasis (that fit hand in glove with the democratic administration ideology). The identification of subject matter sources might reasonably be interpreted as a voice preparing the way for what was to (and did) come.

Wahlquist (1952) recognizes AASA activity and the inception of NCPEA in 1947 as important stirrings in the field. Moore cites those as two of the three significant events that started the ferment that surfaced in the literature after 1954—the third was a recommendation made to the Kellogg Foundation from its education advisory committee that educational administration deserved support (Griffiths, 1964, p. 15; Moore, 1951, chapter 1). These converging forces led to the formulation and implementation of the Cooperative Program in Educational Administration in the 1950–1951 academic year, the Committee for the Advancement of School Administration in 1955, and the University Council for Educational Administration in 1956. Out of these crucibles bubbled the brew that was to become known concurrently as the behavior science and the theory-and-research movement in educational administration.

SUMMARY

Only now with 20/20 hindsight can the textbook literature of the 1946–1954 period be seen as the beginning of a search for a new science (scientific management was the first) of educational administration—a search for which planning was well under way as the period ended. Given the pervasive commitment to democratic ideology and its attendant community focus (the neighborhood school as the melting pot in American society), the difficulties of making that work, and the attention the public schools received as they grew in size and complexity, it is not surprising this search was undertaken. That textbooks neither led the search nor signaled its presence may merely be a commentary on the nature of textbooks—especially in a field so diverse yet common as educational administration, and, most especially, in the early stages of the development of a field of study.

REFERENCES

Adams, H. P., and Dickey, F. G. (1953). *Basic principles of supervision.* New York: American Book Co.

American Association of School Administrators (AASA). (1947). *Schools for a new world. Twenty-fifth yearbook of the AASA.* Washington, D.C.: Author.

AASA. (1955). *Staff relations in school administration. Thirty-third yearbook of the AASA.* Washington, D.C.: Author.

Bartky, J. A. (1953). *Supervision as human relations.* Boston: Heath.

Boardman, D. W., Douglass, K. R., and Bent, R. K. (1953). *Democratic supervision in secondary schools.* Boston: Houghton Mifflin.

Briggs, T. H. (1952). *Improving instruction through supervision.* New York: Macmillan.

Campbell, C. M. (1952). *Practical applications of democratic administration.* New York: Harper.

Campbell, R. F. (1972). Educational administration: a twenty-five year perspective. *Education Administration Quarterly* 8 (Spring): 1–25.

Campbell, R. F., and Gregg, R. T. (eds.). (1957). *Administrative behavior in education.* New York: Harper and Brothers.

Dougherty, J. H. (1950). *Elementary school organization and management.* Rev. ed. New York: Macmillan.

Douglass, K. R. (1954). *Modern administration of secondary schools.* Boston: Ginn.

Edmondson, J. B., Roemer, J., and Bacon, F. L. (1953). *The administration of the modern secondary school.* New York: Macmillan.

Elsbree, W. S., and McNally, H. J. (1951). *Elementary school administration and supervision.* New York: American Book Co.

Elsbree, W. S., and Reutter, E. (1954). *Staff personnel in the public schools.* New York: Prentice Hall.

Fox, James H. (1949). *School administration: principles and procedures.* New York: Prentice-Hall.

Greider, C., and Rosenstengel, W. E. (1954). *Public school administration.* New York: Ronald.

Griffiths, D. E. (ed.). (1964). *Behavioral science and educational administration. Sixty-third yearbook of the NSSE.* Part 2. Chicago: University of Chicago Press for the Society.

Henry, N. B. (ed.). (1954). *Changing conceptions in educational administration. Forty-fifth yearbook of the NSSE.* Part 2. Chicago: University of Chicago Press for the Society.

Henry, N. B. (ed.). (1959). *Community education: Principles and practices from worldwide experience. Fifty-eighth yearbook of the NSSE.* Part 1. Chicago: University of Chicago Press for the Society.

Henry, N. B. (ed.). (1953). *The community school. Fifty-second yearbook of the NSSE.* Part 2. Chicago: University of Chicago Press for the Society.

Hilton, E. (1949). *Rural school management.* New York: American Book Co.

Immegart, G. L. (1975). *The study of educational administration 1954–74: Myths, paradoxes, facts, and prospects.* Paper prepared for the Ohio State University UCEA Career Development Seminar, April.

Knight, E. W. (1953). *Readings in educational administration.* New York: Holt.

Lawson, D. E. (1953). *School administration.* New York: Odyssey Press.

Melby, E. O. (1955). *Administering community education.* Englewood Cliffs: Prentice-Hall.

Melchoir, W. T. (1950). *Instructional supervision: a guide to modern practice.* Boston: Heath.

Moehlman, A. B. (1951). *School administration.* Boston: Houghton Mifflin.

Moore, H. A. (1957). *Studies in school administration: a report on the CPEA.* Washington, D.C.: AASA.

Mort, P. R. (1946). *Principles of school administration: A synthesis of basic concepts.* New York: McGraw-Hill.

Otto, H. J. (1946). *Organizational and administrative practices in elementary schools in the United States.* Austin: University of Texas.

Otto, H. J. (1954). *Elementary school organization and administration.* 3rd ed. New York: Appleton-Century-Crofts.

Ovsiew, L. (1953). *Emerging practices in school administration.* New York: Metropolitan School Study Council and Cooperative Program in Education Administration.

Pittinger, B. R. (1951). *Local public school administration.* New York: McGraw-Hill.

Reavis, W. C. (1946). *Educational administration.* Chicago: University of Chicago Press.

Reavis, W. C. (1954). *Administering the elementary school—A cooperative educational enterprise.* New York: Prentice Hall.

Reeder, W. G. (1951). *The fundamentals of public school administration.* 3rd ed. New York: Macmillan.

Sears, J. B. (1947). *Public school administration.* New York: Ronald.

Sears, J. B. (1950). *The nature of the administrative process.* New York: McGraw-Hill.

Shane, H. G., and Yauch, W. A. (1954). *Creative school administration in elementary and junior high schools.* New York: Holt.

Skogsberg, A. H. (1950). *Administrative operational patterns.* New York: Metropolitan School Study, Bureau of Publications.

Spears, H. (1953). *Improving the supervision of instruction.* New York: Prentice Hall.

Wahlquist, J. T. (1952). *The administration of public education.* New York: Ronald.

Weber, C. A. (1954). *Personnel problems of school administrations.* New York: McGraw-Hill.

Wiles, K. (1950). *Supervision for better schools.* New York: Prentice Hall.

Yauch, W. A. (1949). *Improving human relations in school administration.* New York: Harper.

Yeager, W. A. (1949). *Administration and the pupil.* New York: Harper.

Yeager, W. A. (1954). *Administration and the teacher.* New York: Harper.

6

Factualism to Theory, Art to Science: School-Administration Texts, 1955–1985

Thomas E. Glass

In the early 1950s a considerable number of education administrators began to search for a unique theory of administration. Many practicing administrators and professors had been exposed to the rapidly expanding body of behavioral and social science theory. Conceivably, it would not be difficult to transfer a portion of this theory to the field of educational administration. Additionally, through empirical research new theory particularized to the practice of school administration could be appended to form a new and unique theory of educational administration.

This new theory base was to provide practitioners as well as researchers with the tools of scientific inquiry necessary to understand the phenomena of administering schools. The traditional emphasis on "what is" versus "what ought to be" did not provide administrators an adequate tool to describe, explain, and predict phenomena associated with leading educational institutions. Most early enthusiasts for development of a unique educational-administration theory were professors of educational administration. However, several prominent sociologists and social psychologists at prestigious universities entered the writing in the field.

The reality of the nuclear age, the baby boom, and changing philosophies in society had done much by 1955 to change forever the structure of many social institutions, including the school. The traditional role of the school as the dispenser of basic skills for the masses with limited advanced academic training for the minority had been radically changed as high school graduation rates climbed and increasing numbers of high school graduates attended colleges and universities. Also, a burgeoning technology was working alongside societal changes to produce a school system of increased complexity, necessitating a management system that extended beyond the repeated application of taxonomies of school management principles. The evolving complex society required management and conceptual tools designed to lead large groups of students and staff in a task of formal socialization to a changing technological world. The little red schoolhouse in the country was fast becoming a relic of the past. And, the schoolmaster who kept school had finally been replaced with an administrator who managed extensive human and fiscal resources in the institution known as the school.

The 1950s also saw a virtual explosion of textbooks in educational administration. Especially in the second half of the decade, the number of titles increased rapidly, and the 1960s brought a significant number of general texts, as well as a specialized type. The 1960s produced roughly three times the number of titles as the 1950s. The 1970s continued the rapid publication pace of texts, which tailed off in the 1980s with recession in the economy and, perhaps, a recession in academic production in educational administration.

FACTUALISM TO THEORY IN TEXTBOOKS

In the quarter-century between 1955 and 1980, a clear trend is discernable from the factualism found in compendiums of principles toward a quest for theory and theory application. However, this does not mean that all text writers quickly and fully adopted the new theoretical movement dominated by professors influenced by behavioral and social science research and theory. Such is not the case, and even into the late 1970s and 1980s, some writers only grudgingly acquiesced to social science–inspired administrative theory. Administrative theory often lay side by side with age-old principles of school management and cookbook recipes in many general textbooks.

In fact, the still current philosophical division (practice versus theory) of educational-administration programs in higher education, as well as in the literature, began to develop during the early part of this period. As social science theory began to invade the teachings of many professors of educational administration, others resisted "impractical theories" as being retardants to training successful administrators. The lack of communication between the two groups, as well as an appreciation of both for theory and practical training, led to serious divisive factionalism in many educational-administrator preparation programs.

This has been especially true since the development of the specialized field of educational-policy studies. In many textbooks the line between policy and administration has become very unclear. In fact many former departments of educational administration are currently renamed departments of educational-policy studies and still train and certify administrators.

In brief, the quest for the development of educational theory and its application to school management has, in many respects, been a divisive event. However, administrative philosophies of what "ought to be" were destined in a scientific and high-technology age to be replaced by a quasi-scientific approach. Today, the conflict among professors of educational administration is not about the legitimacy of theory, but whether or not students should be primarily taught "about" administration or "to do" administration. In what doses and in what environmental settings they are taught to lead are often the source of conflict.

In the years between 1955 and 1985, educational administration was clearly in transition from the traditional orthodoxy of the implementation of a set of principles elucidated in "bibles" to a base of theoretical inquiry regarding the organization of the school. However, the ascendancy of organization theorists was not, and is not, total in the textbook literature.

In reviewing and assessing the textbook literature during the 1955–1985 period, the importance of emerging administrative theory cannot be overstated. This movement decidedly did change the content and approach of the leading textbooks.

The selection of texts as being representative of the thirty years covered in this chapter was a long and arduous task due to several complicating factors, one being the existence of many in multiple editions. There was also the problem of numerous high-quality texts in narrowly defined topic areas. Considering the sizable number of volumes available for potential review, several decisions were made to make the task manageable.

First, a decision was made to restrict the review in this chapter to general-type texts in educational administration that might be used in the first stages of administration programs. Again, it must be noted, this chapter is a review and analysis of textbook literature and not of specialized scholarly works.

From a general review of over a hundred texts of all types, it was found that general texts supported the hypothesis that there was a movement from factualism to theory-based administration. Importantly, a decision was made to exclude from review and analysis specialized texts such as those found in policy, law, finance, community relations, personnel, supervision, and planning. Generally, the specialized texts were technical types of works, oftentimes with a theoretical base borrowed from another discipline, their prime audience being administrators concerned with a specific role or task in administration.

This is not to say that such works are not important—they are—but a demarcation line had to be established, and with only several exceptions, they are not mentioned in this chapter. Such is also the case with scholarly types of works that are mentioned only within the context of influencing a general-type text.

CRITERIA USED TO SELECT TEXTS FOR REVIEW

I used three general criteria to select the dozen textbooks reviewed here: first, a consensus among colleagues queried as to what were the important works of the period; second, the actual numbers of volumes sold in their various editions; and third, those seeming to have a significant effect on the profession and its practice. Again, a thesis is advanced that a definite trend toward the use of administrative theory can be found in the period's general textbooks, along with fewer compendiums of principles. In brief, there is increased emphasis in texts to describe, explain, and predict administrative roles and actions.

As mentioned earlier, over a hundred works were surveyed to reach the final list of twelve representative works for detailed analysis. It is certain the selected texts will not meet with the approval of all scholars as being the best leading and representative works of the period. This of course is a matter of personal preference; however, the twelve do represent major publishing trends. Many have been published in multiple editions, denoting a staying power. Professors using the texts often base a text adoption upon their own biases. This might mean a professor in educational administration, not being a strong adherent or proponent of theory application, might choose a text more based in factualism and practical administration. The review includes texts that represent traditionalist and theory types.

The theory-laden texts for the most part were not widely adopted across the country. However, they significantly influenced later works by other authors. Lastly, recognition is given to two books that are not readily assigned the label of general texts in administration. These are brief works on theory and likely provided the inspiration for a large number of later theory texts between 1955 and 1985. They are not included among the selected dozen.

In my opinion the works reviewed are representative of the field of educational administration during its era of greatest expansion and development. In chronological order the texts selected are as follows:

Van Miller, George Madden, and Joseph Kincheloe. (1952). *The Public Administration of American School Systems.*

Calvin Grieder, Thomas Pierce, and E. Forbis Jordan. (1969, 1961, 1954). *Public School Administration.* Edgar Morphet, Roe Johns, and Theodore Reller. (1982, 1974, 1967, 1959). *Educational Administration and Organization.*

Steven Kenezevich. (1984, 1975, 1969, 1962). *Administration of Public Education.*

Roald Campbell et al. (1985, 1975, 1970 1965). *The Organization and Control of American Schools.*

Jacob Getzels, James Lipham, and Roald Campbell. (1968). *Educational Administration As a Social Process.*

Thomas Sergiovanni and Fred D. Carver. (1973). *The New School Executive.*

William Monahan (ed.). (1975). *Theoretical Dimensions of Educational Administration.*

Ralph Kimbrough and Michael Nunnery. (1976). *Educational Administration: An Introduction.*

Wayne Hoy and Cecil Miskel. (1982). *Educational Administration: Theory, Research, and Practice.*

Clarence Newell. (1978). *Human Behavior in Educational Administration.*

Michael Hanson. (1984, 1979). *Educational Administration and Organizational Behavior.*

The reader can see that many of the twelve works have appeared in multiple editions. Sometimes the revisions made between editions have been
substantial and sometimes not. Often, the original author has picked up
coauthors in later editions. In some cases, original authors produced later
editions with a coauthor and then branched off into a new work in the
field at a later time. Whether or not a text has been printed in multiple
editions is largely determined by the philosophical position of the particular educational-administration programs adopting the text. A guess would
be that theoretical works significantly based in the social and behavioral
sciences would be most used in programs directed at the graduate student
later expected to become a researcher or professor, not a practitioner.
However, this is probably not true in all cases. Obviously, the professor
trained and interested in social science theory would more often than not
choose a more academic rather than practical text.

Also, perhaps an educational-administration program at a smaller institution, primarily concerned with the training of master's level students,
might be less interested in a text based in social science theory. Again,
the professor's academic background and the program's direction might
dictate text selection and subsequent sale revenue. During the period from
1955 to 1985, the number of educational-administration students in non-
research institutions greatly outnumbered those in prestigious universities.
This assuredly affected the sales of traditional-type texts.

MOVING AWAY FROM RHETORIC

The previous chapter emphasizes a return to rhetoric, including the con-
tention that democratic themes and community became dominant in textbook literature after World War II. Indeed, the graduate students in educational administration in the 1950s were subject to what might be called a
bit of educational propaganda, but still evident was the trend toward cookbooks and taxonomies of good practices. However, there was a bit of stir-
ring toward development of theory. These initial quests for an administrative theory base are found in Sears and Mort, two very popular authors of

the 1940s and 1950s. Sears in *The Nature of the Administration Process* (1950) ascribes his "concept of administrative theory" mainly to the field of business.

Sears indicates that by studying administrative functions and processes, organizational assumptions can be developed leading to an optimum direction for the organization. His several popular works cannot be labeled compendiums of preferred practices; in fact, the titles use the word "nature." Perhaps this might have been better described as "psychology." To read Sears is to read the contemporary management works of the period such as Chester Barnard's *Function of the Executive,* which, even though published in 1938, furnished most of the basis for management study until that field, too, became heavily impacted by behavioral science theory.

Sears most definitely was a devotee of contemporary management school thought of the period as applied to the school organization. His work had a significant impact on many graduate students in terms of sparking their interest in studying the school management function from the perspective of quasi-organizational theory.

Another strong emphasis in educational administration for a long time was the work of Paul Mort, whose commonsense approach reflected the era in which he worked. In general, he advocates strongly and eloquently a system of value concepts. In his best-known work, *Principles of School Administration* (1957) (the emphasis being on principles), a system of fourteen principles is discussed in great detail, including reasons why they should be implemented in the management of schools. Mort, too, probably unknowingly, was sowing the seeds of administrative theory with his selection of techniques, called principles, which, if tried, would be effective tools of administration. Even though the works of Sears and Mort have been assessed in earlier sections of this book, it is still important to mention that they were still strong influences on the textbook literature. And, the preceding two works forecasted what was to come very shortly to the field of administrative thought and publication.

It is reasonable to assume a three-to-five-year lag between innovation in a field and its appearance in general textbook literature. Thus, events occurring in educational administration in 1955 would not be reflected in the textbook literature until about 1960. This was indeed the case as several crucial events occurred in the 1955–1960 period that later affected the direction and content of many texts published in the 1970s and 1980s.

In 1955, the Kellogg Foundation awarded the University of Chicago a large grant for the development of a program to research and develop a body of theory applicable to the administration of public schools. The task of developing a theory base of administration was also initiated at the same time by a group of faculty at George Peabody College. Soon these groups were sponsoring meetings and seminars for the exchange of ideas and papers. Also, key members of the centers began producing works that would several years later evolve into educational-administration texts.

Among the early theorists were Daniel Griffiths of Teachers College and Andrew Halpin of the Claremont Graduate School. Griffiths, especially, might be referred to as the true father of educational administrative theory. His thin 1959 work entitled *Administrative Theory,* although not a primary general text, has been required reading for thousands of graduate students. Although it is not included among the twelve general texts reviewed here, a strong case can be made that its impact as a secondary or supplemental text has been substantial. In this small book Griffiths traces the history of attempts to develop theory in administration and, more importantly, to define what theory is, is not, and should be in educational administration (Griffiths, 1959).

Griffiths outlines the steps necessary for the development of theory and how it should be used in research and day-to-day administration. He later expands on his outline of theory and its impact on decision making in *Administrative Theory in Education* (1958), a collection of papers edited by Andrew Halpin. This second of what might be called basic books on the road to administrative theory developed out of a conference held at the University of Chicago in 1957 under the aegis of the then newly formed University Council for Education Administration, along with the Midwest Administration Center, already mentioned as being the vehicle for the Kellogg Grant to the University of Chicago (Halpin, 1958).

In the first chapter in *Administrative Theory in Education* (1958), Halpin explains the need for and value of administrative theory. He also asks those in educational administration who are not enamored with theory as the basis for study and application to give it a fair hearing. He never says the purpose is to develop a single administrative theory to dictate practice (p. 4).

He also makes a key point that one of the most significant uses of theory in educational administration in future decades will be to develop testable hypotheses (p. 5). Today, probably a majority of doctoral dissertations in educational administration are exercises in testing a theory base.

In brief, Halpin's lead article in the book is a call for the development and use of theory in administration. In his opinion, administrators could accomplish this, both in the field and in higher education, becoming quasi–social scientists. They should constantly utilize appropriate methodology and tools to test hypotheses of practice.

Halpin candidly describes the difficulties encountered in developing theory in administration, which reappear in the final chapter, written by Roald Campbell, which states what the three main purposes of schools should be: (1) developing critical thinking skills, (2) establishing basic literacy, and (3) providing a vehicle for social mobility (Halpin, p. 71). Campbell cites all of the problem areas in educational administration that make it difficult, if not impossible, to draw general conclusions regarding wide-ranging theories. Interestingly, he sometimes slips into a "what ought to be" voice (pp. 168–185).

Administrative Theory in Education is included in this review because it was the work of the Midwest Conference (UCEA) that had a significant impact on subsequent authors of administration texts. Halpin, in a later book entitled *Theory and Research in Administration* (1966), took what his publishers declared to be the new movement in the training of educational administrators a step further, attempting to provide the field with a textbook in pure educational-administration theory. The result was an interesting book, but certainly not a general text. However, its scholarly nature is evident, and Halpin, along with Griffiths, provides the impetus for future text writers, following their lead in emphasizing theory and the use of the tools of social and behavioral science.

A juncture is now apparent in the development of general textbooks. Griffiths, Halpin, and others are the impetus for change and the use of theory in administration. Did text writers heed their call for a more scientific approach to administration? And, more importantly, did practitioners heed the call and begin to think not only of managing buildings and districts, but also about how as social scientists they might change organizational structure and behaviors? The first question is answered to a degree by examining a representative number of textbooks. The second question is far more difficult to answer with any degree of certainty and is perhaps best left to other writers addressing theory influencing administrative roles and behaviors.

THREE TRENDS FOUND IN TEXTBOOKS

The dozen general-type textbooks reviewed can be placed in one of three trends or categories:

1. A strong emphasis on theory development and the use of social and behavioral science tools, models, techniques, and methodologies
2. A reliance on time-proven principles, taxonomies, and versions of "what is" versus "what ought to be," the traditional approach of opinion
3. A mixture of the traditional versus the emerging administrative science based on the social and behavioral sciences, which may be viewed as willing or grudging mergers.

The reader should be aware that chronology is not necessarily a significant factor in determining a text's trend or category.

Along with Mort and Sears, Van Miller of the University of Illinois was a very popular text writer during the 1950s and 1960s. His approach in *The Public Administration of American School Systems* (1952), published by the Macmillan Company, is that of a traditional generalist. The first edition of this book appeared in 1952 with Willard Spalding as a coauthor and reappeared in 1959 with Spalding, in 1965 with Miller as sole author, and again in 1972 with George Madden and James B. Kincheloe as coauthors. One of the reasons this work was selected is its various editions and number of coauthors. Succinctly, the content did change over the years until an almost new book emerged. However, the overall approach did not significantly change from being a good descriptive account of public schools in the United States and how they should be administered. In fact, Miller and Spalding avoid many of the shortcomings of previous writers by never expressly saying what is "good" practice and what is "not good" practice.

They adequately explain the multitude of functions that every school district must perform every day, every week, and every month of the year.

And, when they do make recommendations, they do so in a very tactful and subtle manner. In the 1972, as well as the 1965, edition a final chapter is devoted to discussion of the profession of education administration. In the 1965 edition Miller alone discusses the development of the Midwest Center, the University Council of Education Administration, and other groups attempting to further the professionalism and status of educational administration. By the 1972 edition a chapter is added discussing the development of administrative thought. This is indeed a very long way from the 1952 first edition! Whether Miller wrote this final chapter is questionable, but nonetheless, Miller and his coauthors were conceding to changes in the field. Also, to their credit, they are perfectly honest in the book; they say in an introductory note:

> The text provides the student with a challenging exercise in reconsidering his present information and opinions, in seeking additional information and expert opinion, and in organizing his views into a consistently defensible, though flexible, understanding of the public administration of American school systems. This book is intended to develop a student's overall perspective. It is not a scientific treatise on school administration in the United States, nor is it a guidebook on how to administer schools. (Miller, Madden, and Kincheloe, 1972, pp. iv, v)

Indeed, the book is a collection of subtle opinions, presumably by experts, who have tried out the practices expressed in the school environments so well described. And, most assuredly, the book is not a scientific work based on sound theory, explanation of phenomena, and predictive postulates. However, to dismiss this book as having little value would be inappropriate. The last chapter does describe then current trends in theory development and does not pretend to be what it is not. Most importantly, it is essential for practicing, as well as potential, administrators to read the function descriptions and the expert opinions contained in such works.

There is a place in the literature for descriptive writing, perhaps more so than for expert opinions. Function analysis is legitimate, and that performed in Van Miller's principal work is well done and should still be of interest today. It is no wonder the book in its many editions was widely used and served as a replacement for previous texts by Sears, Mort, and Cubberley. Of the three categories it can be classed as traditional, even with the chapter regarding the development of management theory. The role of the social sciences does not emerge, but nonetheless the new movement of Halpin did, if in a small way, impact the last edition.

The next work reviewed is a three-edition text widely used particularly in Midwestern schools in the late 1950s and 1960s, *Public School Administration* (1969) by Calvin Grieder, Truman Pierce, and K. Forbis Jordan. This book must have been a favorite of the traditionalists as it is a descriptive work with pages and pages of expert opinion. Where Van Miller's function descriptions were extensive, these authors spend far less time in describing functions and problems associated with performance and practice. This book is largely a commonsense approach to administration, as so long advocated by Sears. The expert opinion approach is squarely the overall theme. It tells a little bit about an extensive array of tasks and functions that must be performed in a school district. Opinions expressed by the authors include such platitudes as that they firmly believe the school district board has proved to be one of the chief contributors to the progress of education and that it should be preserved and strengthened. Who can argue with that expert opinion?

This book is the most elementary of the dozen works surveyed and the one falling most easily into the traditionalist category. It was selected primarily because of its three editions and popularity. It is easily readable by a novice in educational administration. It is divided into major fields of administration and exemplifies exactly a general work of the period. In summary, it is more "cookbookish" than texts written by Jesse Sears and Van Miller.

Perhaps the most classic of all texts that are nontheory oriented, but descriptive, telling the most about educational administration, is the all-time best-seller in the field, *Educational Organization and Administration: Concepts, Practices, and Issues*, by Edgar L. Morphet, Roe L. Johns, and Theodore L. Reller. The four editions of this work were printed between 1959 and 1982. In the twenty-three years that the book was in print, it was widely used across the nation. As I understand it, more copies were sold than of any of Elwood Cubberley's single volumes. The format and the purpose of the text stayed constant, but the content changed. As concepts, practices, and issues changed, so did *Educational Organizations and Administration*. For example the 1974 edition contained a chapter on accountability, a hot issue in education in the 1970s.

A chapter on collective bargaining in the last two editions also reflects attempts to keep the text current. However, this very important contribution to the field of textbook literature does not pretend to advance the cause of theory. The third edition mentions the importance of theory development by saying, "The practice of education administration, as well as of administration in general, is becoming more scientific because the body of pertinent knowledge is being increased by scientific study" (pp. 14–15). It goes on to say that development of theory or theories of administration are bringing new ideas, knowledge, and understanding to the field. In chapter 3, a treatment of systems theory as applied to administration is offered, as are citations from works of Getzels, Coladarci, Etzioni, Parsons, Prethus, Gouldner, and other organizational theorists either in the social sciences or in education.

This attempt at updating an essentially descriptive text to one that melds theory and description is successful as far it goes. The authors modified the work but did not essentially change the primary thrust of description and selective expert opinion. It is no wonder the work weathered the surges and fluctuations in education administration. It subtly changed with the times and still furnishes a valuable service to the profession by furnishing one of the best overall pictures of administrative functions and processes of that day. One wonders if the authors ever considered teaming *Educational Organization and Administration* with a theory-grounded text. The classification for Morphet, Johns, and Reller would decidedly be in the middle category of a moderate synthesis between theory and tradition.

A work close to the content and quality of *Educational Organization and Administration* is *Administration of Public Education* by Stephen Knezevich. This very widely adopted text appeared in 1984 in its fourth edition. It was first published in 1962 and was periodically updated by Knezevich until his death. The content is more consistent than that of Morphet, Johns, and Reller. It is more statistically oriented than any other of the twelve books reviewed, is of the second category of books, and, overall, may be the most practically theory oriented. This is especially true in the third and fourth editions, which advance organizational theory found in the fields of sociology, psychology, and political science. Included are theory tools, their descriptions, and how they might be applied to solving educational problems.

Leadership theory also emerges in the text in a very coherent manner that is easily understandable by a layperson, let alone a graduate student or practicing administrator. Strangely, leadership theory for a profession grounded in leadership is not the focus of many of the reviewed texts. Interestingly enough, Knezevich approaches from the standpoint of a moderate treatment of theory, then moves into a more descriptive treatment of the school organization and structure, and concludes with policy issues.

This is was a well-organized and well-structured basic text with much to recommend it to either the professor or the student desiring to know something about administrative theory as well as the more practical aspects of school leadership. It is an almost perfect blend of theory and practicality. It most definitely shows the influence of theorists and social scientists working both in and out of colleges of education. Also, it is probably the multiedition text that underwent the fewest changes between editions.

Another standard text, published in five editions, was *The Organization and Control of American Schools* by Roald Campbell, Luvern L. Cunningham, Raphael O. Nystrand, Michael D. Usdan, and other coauthors in later editions. Each of the reviewed texts has a point of emphasis, and *The Organization and Control of American Schools* leans more toward a description and explanation of organs of governance than other texts. This book more than others focuses on governance issues found in education and advances some ways to resolve or meet these challenges. The third, fourth, and fifth editions are updates, but do not dramatically change the overall format of the work. In fact, only small changes could be found in a scanning of all five editions. The first edition appeared in 1965 and the last in 1985.

The use of theory is minimal in Campbell and Cunningham and appears only infrequently, as, for instance, Egon Guba's model of internal administration is discussed accompanied by charts and graphs. Again, this book focuses on control and legal and statistical descriptions of the governance process. In addition, extensive treatment is given to external change agent groups such as communities, governmental agencies, and colleges. Each edition of the book furnished interesting statistics on many groups such as teachers and students.

This work might be said to be among the first policy-directed texts. Its strong emphasis on governance, educational client groups, and descriptions of how schools are governed more than administered provides an excellent example of a beginning work in educational-policy studies. Campbell and Cunningham perhaps unknowingly were branching off the mainstream of general educational administration into a more specialized field. However, the influence of the social and behavioral sciences and theoretical base is not apparent in this work. It has to be classified as a traditionalist work, just a bit removed from the mainstream of general textbook literature in the field.

TEXTS HEAVILY BASED IN THEORY

The next reviewed work, *Educational Administration As a Social Process: Theory Research and Practice,* by Jacob Getzels, James Lipham, and Roald Campbell, first published in 1968, is the most radical departure from the mainstream of the literature for a decade. This is probably the first text in administration to strongly emphasize theory and social science research at the cost of not spending hundreds of pages describing the general educational enterprise and its myriad of challenges and problems. This book was indeed a radical departure and probably was not used as an introductory text in many colleges and universities. Of its three authors it seems likely that Getzels and Lipham wrote most of the book. Getzels likely contributed most of the theoretical structures, and Lipham contributed chapters dealing with subjects such as staff and board relationships. In this work, Roald Campbell and his colleagues do what few other text writers of this period were able to do, namely, make a total transition from description to theory.

The work is structured much as might be expected of a theory text with a secondary emphasis on research and practice. The content of theory is first discussed before moving to development of administrative theory and how it might be applied to educational administration. Next, the most often cited part of the book is Getzel and Guba's "nomothetic and idiographic dimensions" of personnel administration. Subsequent chapters deal in great detail with the context of culture in administration, institutional expectations, roles, conflict, and personal needs. Truly, the book attempts to look at theory, the institution, the person, and how the three can be moved toward institutional, as well as individual, goals. A great deal of time is spent on role definition, role conflict, and institutionalization. The reader may feel the book is in the field of social psychology until the final chapters, when specific school-oriented functions, roles, and problems are encountered.

Staff relations, the role of school boards, teacher organizations, and relations with the community are discussed, and relevant research is cited that pertains to current issues in those areas, but with a social science theory base. To say the least, this book borrows heavily from the social and behavioral sciences and does not apologize. It truly is a pioneering work, a bit clumsy in places, hard to read in others, but in total a good effort to develop a theory of administration and put it to work in understanding the school institution.

This does not mean the book is without fault. It most certainly should be criticized for some of its hard-to-read passages. And, it is certainly difficult to put into clear, concise English the theories of Talcott Parsons.

This book first reached the field in 1968 and followed the publication of Halpin's *Administrative Theory in Education* after the 1957 Midwest Conference at the University of Chicago. Unfortunately, Getzels and Lipham were unable to have their book published within several years after the important theory conferences of the late 1950s. This would have surely brought more attention to and and perhaps induced use of their theory-based general text.

A second theory-based general administration text following Getzels and Lipham's was *The New School Executive. A Theory of Administration*, written in 1973 by Thomas Sergiovanni and Fred Carver, both at the University of Illinois. The work is brief for a general text closely focused on administrative theory for school executives. In the textbook literature this is the first extensive use of the term *school executive*. The book leans toward the superintendency and establishes a precedent for a later division in texts addressing generic building and central office administration. Prior to this text the superintendency and principalship were described in role textbooks. Today, much of the literature on the superintendency defines the role as that of chief executive officer.

Writing five years after the Getzels and Lipham, Sergiovanni and Carver had time to further synthesize and incorporate then current theory and research from sociology and psychology into an educational-administration context. Their borrowings are most appropriate and valuable. The orientation of the book is decidedly behavioral and fits the trend to promote an administrative emphasis to loosen bureaucratic structures and find ways by which staff, students, and parents can be treated in humane ways.

Interestingly, Sergiovanni and Carver are concerned with what they call a "belief system," meaning values, attitudes, goals, and objectives. The first half of the book is primarily focused on the individual within the institution. Motivation, adjustment, satisfaction, and ways of decision making are certainly approached from the viewpoint of a social psychologist concerned with the health of a productive organization. Sergiovanni and Carver borrow from McGregor, Maslow, and Herzberg, among other behavioral scientists, in a well-organized manner. In brief, they attempt to use social-psychology research to explain contemporary situations and problems in school management, and to reinforce what they think to be the best approaches to conflict resolution.

Also, the first half of the book is a discussion of values and what might be called a discussion of a moral philosophy for the new school executive, who the authors feel should be a quasi-social-behavioral scientist. The authors probably thought at the time that administrators were not utilizing the benefits and contributions of management science at work in the private sector. To say the least, they create a dichotomy by boldly stating that the field should be a science and at the same time introducing subjects that might be classified as "practical strategies." However, this is not a serious failing of the work, as it is difficult to differentiate between a proposed action based on assumption, theory, and hypothesis versus a commonsense practice.

The second half of the book primarily deals with organizational aspects of management. The administrator is renamed "the school executive." The workplace, environment, subordinate relationships, and leadership style are all briefly discussed within the context of the research findings and theoretical models of Egon Cuba, Jacob Getzels, Andrew Halpin, and others. If this book is to be criticized, it is from the perspective that a synthesis of social psychology and management science transferred to educational leadership is not appropriate for a general text in educational administration.

Of the texts reviewed, *The New School Executive* is among those with the fewest pages. It definitely fits in the category of a specialized general text emphasizing a theory approach. It is basically a reexamination of other works and is exactly the opposite of the traditionalists' approach. It is in many respects an extension of Getzels and Lipham's *Educational Administration As a Social Process.*

Of the selected dozen texts, the only one classified as the "edited type" is *Theoretical Dimensions of Educational Administration* assembled by William Monahan (1975). Most texts containing a series of papers or monographs by a group of authors were generally rather disjointed, without a constant approach and purpose. However, William Monahan's *Theoretical Dimensions of Educational Administration* is interesting because it approaches the same task that Sergiovanni and Carver did, using its authors in a different way; for instance, several contributors are noneducators.

The book is very effective in identifying the main concerns of education requiring the development of administrative theory. The content and scope of the work are impressive, and the quality of the writings superb, and it probably was never among the best-sellers. Of the reviewed works, it fits most solidly into the theory category.

Monahan is really the only total theory work called a general text in educational administration. Although one may disagree with Monahan, who states in the preface that the book is an introductory text, it is a bit heavy for entry-level graduate students. Among the contributors are Egon Guba, Andrew Halpin, James Anderson, Warren Bennis, B. Jean Hills, and Robert Nisbet. This is an interesting text but is now outdated. In many respects it is the oddball of the dozen and the most difficult to read, along with Getzels and Lipham. Nonetheless, Monahan has a clear idea as to the development of theory and its relation to school organization and climate.

Ralph B. Kimbrough and Michael Y. Nunnery, in *Educational Administration: An Introduction,* return to the traditionalist approach of description with a bit of expert opinion. This book, published in 1976, is in some respects a return to the old standards like Morphet and Johns. Even though the authors claim a total integration of theory and practice, providing a general overview of administration, I note only several chapters summarizing leading schools of thought in organizational theory. In addition, other chapters focusing on community, governance, district politics, and collective bargaining are very traditionalistic. To be fair, the authors have taken traditionalist description and blended it with current social science theory. However, the format of identifying areas of normal school function and then seeking a relevant social-behavioral science theory to fit is not necessarily helpful.

The reader might think it would be more productive to dispense with the book and instead buy two texts, one such as Morphet and Johns that provides the description of administrative functions and perhaps one by Peter Drucker providing organization and management theory. Thus, the educationist could gain a more in-depth understanding from two leading authors in their respective fields of inquiry. As the middle-category works go, this book is not ideal but acceptable.

This text by 1990 had not appeared in a second edition, which was somewhat surprising, as I thought this type of new movement compendium would be popular with professors of educational administration in many programs classified as middle of the road between theory and practice emphasis.

In *Educational Administration: Theory, Research, and Practice* (1982), Wayne Hoy and Cecil Miskel (later joined by Patrick Forsythe) provide perhaps the best integration of research findings and administrative theory. The authors very carefully weave research findings by Fred Fiedler, Amitai Etzioni, Thomas Sergiovanni, Frederick Herzberg, and others into a rationale for how and why they are important to theory development and operational practice. Many graduate students will find the going difficult in some of the chapters, but overall the book does an excellent job of summarizing contemporary organizational and leadership theory, along with making suggestions for practical applications.

This book is without doubt one of the better theory-oriented books, and at the same time has something of interest and benefit to the practitioner-oriented student. It clearly falls in the theory group, and new editions might simplify several chapters and expand discussion of practical application in field settings.

Clarence Newell's text entitled *Human Behavior in Educational Administration* (1978) might be questioned as to being among leaders in textbook literature in educational administration. However, it falls among the period's general-type texts, appearing in its first edition. The text was selected because it exemplified an emerging pattern of multiple texts being used in general administration courses. It is not large (261 pages) and provides a direct focus on human behavior in the school organization. It too repeats or reexamines leading theorists and researchers fairly and without losing context. The strongest feature of the book is its treatment of the communication process so important for effective practice. In some respects, of the selected dozen, this text best attempts to provide the reader with empirical data tied closely to implementing social science theory in administrative practice.

In some ways it approaches a how-to type of work. Its weak points are that it is often superficial and brief and does not cover a wide spectrum, as do many other texts. Its focus is rather narrow and as a dollar-for-dollar investment cannot stand up to other general texts. However, it is a good supplementary text when an instructor wishes to have two different books serve as one general text. An argument might be made that today's complex technological world, coupled with the advancement of knowledge in the social-behavioral sciences, prevents one single text from adequately furnishing an overall picture of school management. It is for this reason that *Human Behavior in Educational Administration* is included in the reviewed group.

The last book reviewed is *Educational Administration and Organizational Behavior* (1984) by Mark Hanson. This is a very interesting text from the standpoint of content and organization. It was first published in 1979 and was used in many programs across the country. This is definitely the work of a new movement administrator/social psychologist and reflects totally the abandonment of the traditionalist use of description and opinion. In some respects it is amazing, as no other period text uses case study to the degree found in *Educational Administration and Organizational Behavior.*

The work is very efficient; the author reviews rapidly in one chapter classical theory, the contingency theory of leadership, the path-goal theory of leadership, open systems theory, and other situational theories of leadership. In brief, he says a lot in a minimum number of pages.

Surprisingly, of the twelve reviewed books, Hanson's is the only one to devote a chapter to the study of educational change models. Most every reviewed text discussed decision-making models, but neglected the change models being continually adopted to implement reform. For an instructor to cover the content of this book in sixteen to eighteen class meetings over a semester is a heavy task. The merit of the book is the amount of theory and research covered relating directly to the administrative function. The demerits are that it is a general overview and does not provide sufficient depth for a clear, concise picture of the administrative topic in question.

Thus, the often-encountered problem of general textbooks having to be general and specific at the same time to accomplish the end of providing students a wide spectrum of information becomes more difficult. Perhaps, this becomes more daunting as the field becomes more specialized. Hanson's attempt to perform this impossible task is commendable, and the book deserves to be used by instructors desiring a competent overview of how the social sciences impact the administration of schools.

To conclude this review without a parting comment about the excellent texts currently found in specialized areas would be remiss. Within the specialized administrative functions and topic areas such as policy, personnel, supervision, community relations, and law are many excellent texts. Many of these texts are general texts for those specialized areas. For instance, Gordon McCloskey's *Education and Public Understanding* (1958) was for many years the standard work in community relations used around the nation. However, it too was eclipsed in the 1960s because of the application of the social sciences to that specialized area. Texts that discussed minority culture groups found in various urban communities quickly became dominant. The field of school law is replete with casebooks that have been periodically updated as new developments have occurred in that rapidly growing field. Instructional leadership emphasis has transformed texts in supervision to prescriptive tomes. Personnel administration has been dominated for several decades by numerous editions of works by just two authors, William Castetter and Ronald Rebore.

In summary, after a review of leading texts in general education administration, it is apparent that a single volume under four hundred pages simply cannot achieve the multiple task of encompassing the total spectrum of description, explanation, and prediction of school management. Tremendously large or multivolume texts would probably be the answer, but a publisher's taking on a two- or three-volume general text in school administration is unlikely. Also, it is probable that no such manuscript has been or is being produced. Some aspiring set of writers should embark on such a mission!

REFERENCES

Campbell, R., et al. (1985). *The organization and control of American schools.* New York: Harper and Row.

Campbell, R. Peculiarities in educational administration. In Halpin, A. (ed.). *Administrative theory in education.* New York: Macmillan.

Getzels, J., Lipham, J., and Campbell, R. (1968). *Educational administration as a social process.* New York: Harper and Row.

Grieder, C., Pierce, T., and Jordan, F. (1969). *Public school administration.* New York: Macmillan.

Griffiths, D. (1959). *Administrative theory in education.* New York: Appleton-Century-Crofts.

Halpin, A. (ed.). (1958). *Administrative theory in education.* New York: Macmillan.

Hanson, M. (1984). *Educational administration and organizational behavior.* Boston: Allyn and Bacon.

Hoy, W., and Miskel, C. (1982). *Educational administration: theory, practice, and research.* New York: MacGraw-Hill.

Kimbrough, R., and Nunnery, M. (1976). *Educational administration: an introduction.* New York: Macmillan.

Kenezevich, S. (1984). *Administration of public education.* New York: Harper and Row.

Miller, V., Madden, G., and Kincheloe, J. (1972). *The public administration of American school systems.* New York: Harper and Row.

Monahan, W. (ed.). (1975). *Theoretical dimensions of educational administration.* New York: Macmillan.

Morphet, E., Johns, R., and Reller, T. (1982). *Educational administration and organization.* New York: Macmillan.

Mort, P. (1957). *Principles of school administration.* New York: McGraw-Hill.

Newell, C. (1978). *Human behavior in educational administration.* New York: Prentice Hall.

Sears, J. (1950). *The nature of the administrative process.* New York: McGraw-Hill.

Sergiovanni, T., and Carver, F. D. (1973). *The new school executive: a theory of administration.* New York: Harper and Row.

7

A Retreat from Theory in an Era of Reform: 1985–2000

Thomas E. Glass

AN ERA OF REFORM

In 1983, the National Commission on Excellence in Education initiated an era of school reform in its report *A Nation at Risk,* an era characterized by a long and disappointing march toward quality education for all children. Nearly every state by 2000 had embarked on a series of top-down reforms to make public education more effective and accountable. Key top-down reforms are sets of standards and high-stakes tests challenging schools and districts to raise scores or face governmental punishment.

Twenty years of school reform has significantly changed the textbook literature serving the field of educational administration. A movement back to practice-oriented textbooks has occurred in the midst of reformist texts offering silver bullets to cure every conceivable problem in public education. It is an understatement to say that textbook literature between 1985 and 2000 can be classified as theory-oriented or traditional. Course adoptions certainly have become multiple, and reliance on a single generalist text has faded away in most programs. The text likely to be adopted in the reform era depends on what happens to be the hottest issue of the moment.

THE CONTRADICTORY WORLD OF SCHOOL REFORM

A few states between 1985 and 2000 sponsored bottom-up reforms to restructure schools. These reforms from the school level seemingly have had marginal effect on the traditional process of schooling. A focus on reforming classroom teaching and instructional leadership by principals sums up fifteen years of attempts to achieve systemic reform. Reform has featured continuous impressive rhetoric accompanied by unimpressive improvement in test scores and meeting the demands of politicians and citizens to fix societal shortcomings through public school education. A particular disappointment to both reformists and politicians is the inability of large urban school districts to raise test scores. After two decades of reform, these schools remain costly, ineffective, organizationally unstable, and governed by counterproductive board politics.

School-reform literature in this period features not only reform critics, but also critics of the critics. In the late 1980s and early 1990s, many school-reform critics portrayed political opportunism as the driving force behind reform. They pointed out that adequate resources seldom accompanied reform mandates. Many times these mandates were funded through cutbacks or lateral transfers of funds from other programs.

The Reagan Administration especially used school reform as a political tool. Reagan appointees to the U.S. Department of Education used the department as a "bully pulpit," lambasting public education at every opportunity, diverting public and media attention from other social problems, such as urban poverty, unemployment, illiteracy, and inadequate health care. The neoconservative politics in education was pushed through books and articles (often subsidized by conservative foundations) written by William Bennett, Chester Finn, Eric Hanushek, Dennis Doyle and John Chubb. These tracts (many times thinly disguised neoconservative propaganda) were widely circulated, but seldom referenced in educational-administration textbook literature. Certainly, many of these books and articles calling for a revolution in public education were text adoptions in policy and instructional-leadership courses.

The period in public education between 1985 and 2000 may be called an era of political opportunism by "reform" presidents and governors of both political parties. Professional education and educational administration in particular were attacked and put on the defensive. One must wonder if this critical and hostile literature affected the professional esteem and performance of teachers and administrators.

During this period politicians, the popular media, neoconservatives, and opportunistic academics brought schools to the public's attention not for support, but for condemnation. This period of "school bashing" might today be responsible for the shortage of teachers and administrators across the country. Who wants to be part of a discredited profession?

David Tyack and Larry Cuban provide the best view of political attacks (to achieve reform) in *Tinkering toward Utopia: A Century of Public School Reform* (1995). Other scholarly books (not really intended to be general texts) were *The Predictable Failure of Educational Reform* (1990) by Seymour Sarason and *The Manufactured Crisis* (1995) by David Berliner and Bruce Biddle. These quasi-texts were used in educational-policy classes to point out the foibles of the school reformists. Another policy text, David Conley's *Roadmap to Reform* (1993), is actually a cookbook compendium on how to accomplish reform. This and other policy texts during this period often replaced traditional general textbooks because they were of high interest to both professors and students. The movement to splinter policy studies away from educational administration was achieved by reformist (sometimes near "pulp quality") substitutions.

Many efforts resulting in failure and frustration for school reformists appeared from the onset to be conceptually unsound and uninformed about school organizations and cultures. The lessons taught by the old and present general textbooks in educational administration were lost on the reformers. A majority of reform literature was likely written by noneducators of the opinion that educators were not credible enough to be reformers. Unfortunately, too little reform rhetoric provided constructive criticism and advice. A good example of constructive criticism is found in Theodore Sizer's *Horace's School* (1992), where both criticism and prescription are thoughtfully presented. In brief, most educational-reform literature seems to portray educators as part of the problem, rather than part of the solution. There is little discussion by the reformers as to who will implement reform!

Many of the worst reform efforts seeking to achieve educational utopia reflect the hilarious, but serious, themes found in the Laurel and Hardy film *Utopia*. Well-intentioned but uninformed reform efforts advocated by those possessing neither knowledge nor commitment to assume responsibility might best sum up much of the textbook literature of this decade and a half. This fifteen-year period may be seen by future historians not as a great awakening in public education, but a period of destructive, divisive, and counterproductive attempts to make the public schools cure the ills of society.

REFORMING EDUCATIONAL ADMINISTRATION
AND TEXTBOOK LITERATURE

By the early 1990s colleges of education and departments of educational administration, belatedly perhaps, became targets of school reformists and neoconservative critics. Higher-education professionals were lumped together with teachers, principals, and superintendents as part of the problem, rather than part of the solution to changing schools. Again, authors like John Chubb and Terry Moe in *Politics, Markets, and America's Schools* (1990) and Eric Hanushek in *Making Schools Work: Improving Performance and Controlling Costs* (1994) targeted all groups involved in public education.

The educational-administration professoriate, anticipating attacks, responded by forming several national groups guided by the goal of improving the preparation of administrators. In 1989 the National Policy Board for Educational Administration published *Improving Education of School Administrators: An Agenda for Reform,* which touched a raw nerve with many professors. However, the criticism contained in this small book helped set the agenda for initial efforts to better prepare administrators. The national policy board, which comprised representatives of professional groups such as the American Association of School Administrators, the National Council of Professors of Educational Administration, and the University Council on Educational Administration, chastised preparation programs lacking in quality, rigor, and relevance to professional practice. A good summation of how the professoriate reacted to the call for reform is found in *Continuity and Change: The Educational Leadership Professoriate* (1997), written by Martha McCarthy and George Kuh and sponsored by the University Council on Educational Administration.

In most political or professional movements, a critical moment can be identified. In the movement to reform educational-administrator preparation programs, this critical moment occurred in an invited address to Division A (administration) at the annual meeting of the American Education Research Association conference in New Orleans. Daniel Griffiths (1988), a longtime advocate of the theory movement in educational administration, delivered a hard-hitting paper entitled "Educational Administration: Reform PDQ or RIP." He cited a litany of ills afflicting moribund programs and submitted five initiatives to bring about effectiveness in preparing administrators for the world of reform.

Griffith's ultimatum touched off other critiques of preparation programs. Although there were virtually no supporters of educational-administration preparation programs during the 1980s and 1990s, a national study of the superintendency conducted by Thomas Glass, Lars Bjork, and Chris Brunner for AASA in 2000 found superintendents feeling their academic preparation to be of good quality.

The importance of Griffith's ultimatum was that it came from one of the founding fathers (and authors) of the theory movement in educational administration. He did not necessarily recant, but certainly did minimize the importance of the quest for administrative theory. The best source on Griffith and the founding fathers of the theory movement is "A Century's Quest for a Knowledge Base," contributed by Jack Culbertson to the *Handbook on Research in Educational Administration* (1988).

In summary, the drive for the development of an administrative theory was mostly over, and no longer would administrators be expected to be scientists and scholars, as well as practitioners. Thirty years of social and behavioral science emphasis was, at least partially, coming to a close. The question now was whether the professors and textbook authors would change to meet the new realities.

A NEW ERA IN TEXTBOOKS EMERGES

Whether or not Griffith's "PDQ or RIP" paper created a new era in the preparation of administrators is debatable. However, the criticism certainly did affect the textbooks written later in the era. Social movements of the era influencing these texts were multiculturalism, feminism, and religious conservatism. Historically, textbooks in educational administration have been relatively free of politics, but during the reform era, textbooks began to reflect the political correctness of the moment.

Professors have always possessed the authority to select textbooks for their students. Several criteria utilized in exercising this professorial privilege are (1) content, (2) presentation, (3) practicality/usability, (4) cost, (5) compatibility with casebooks, and, recently, (6) licensure standards.

Publishers are sensitive to which texts will sell in significant numbers and conduct extensive surveys to determine whether a manuscript has sales potential sufficient to retrieve its production costs. The real text buyer is the professor rather than the student, who has no option but to purchase the prescribed book.

Again, the two historical types of text in educational administration are (1) general and (2) specialized. This book focuses on the general texts as they serve as a barometer of the times. Although many general texts go through a series of editions, the changes made over the years provide important clues to identifying and understanding influences on practice.

If a professor is enamored with administrative theory, the choice of text may reflect this bias. On the other hand if the interests of the professor are more practitioner-based, then a textbook will be selected with suggestions and strategies for practice. Understanding social and behavioral theory might be framed in the guise of case studies, rather than through the work of researchers in the field.

Many of the theory-based general textbooks published in the 1970s and 1980s replaced the hands-on texts of the 1950s and 1960s. In the early 1990s there was a discernable textbook movement toward more practice and less theory. To be sure, many authors of theory texts started by the early 1990s to adjust to the desires of publishers for a more hands-on approach. The authors sometimes seriously revised the texts. Sometimes, they just added "field-based suggestions" at the ends of chapters and perhaps a new chapter or two on the hot topics of instructional leadership and reform.

TEXTBOOKS MOVE TOWARD
PROBLEMS OF PRACTICE

Between 1985 and 2000 a number of case study textbooks appeared on the market. Publishers strongly recommended adopting them in conjunction with a general text, which presented students with a more expensive text adoption choice. In some institutions the cost of course texts exceeded tuition. Despite the costs, many of the case studies texts provided an opportunity for professors to introduce more realism into their classes. The downside to the case studies books was the problem of maintaining currency. Problems and situations change in public schools. Case studies books existed in the 1960s, but were generally ignored by educational-administration professors.

New interests involving qualitative research accompanied the advent of case studies texts. During this period there was a shift in doctoral dissertations from empirical studies to those using the methodologies of case study, historiography, and ethnography.

THE CHALLENGE OF THE GENERAL TEXTBOOK

The general textbook in educational administration presents many challenges to potential authors. First, it is most often used in an introductory course. Therefore, it must be clear and concise. Second, the book must be readable by classroom teachers. It should relate to the world of the school as seen through their eyes. It must not present an unrealistic picture of educational administration and administrators. Third, it must flow well through a thirteen- to fifteen-week semester. Lastly, it must not cover only the essentials of professional practice, but must also discuss the district governance process, district programs, state agencies, the courts, and the federal government's role in supporting public education. In brief, it must be a composite presentation of theory, practice, and research, perhaps not necessarily in that order.

A comparison of chapter titles suggests that authors model new general texts on earlier published works. Even though few new general texts were published in the 1985–2000 period, the dominant group was substantially based on theory.

A REVIEW OF SELECTED TEXTS

The general textbooks selected for review and discussion are not the only general textbooks in educational administration published in the 1985–2000 period. Many, if not a majority of the texts, were in a second, third, or later editions. A review of previous editions usually reveals significant modification between editions. As in the past, there are continual changes in secondary authors.

Some of the old-time favorites appear again in this chapter after languishing for several decades, while more modern theory texts continued to be used in academically prestigious programs or by professors trained by professor-mentors in research institutions. A contributing factor bringing an end to the theory era was the near disappearance of teacher and administrator certification programs in many major research institutions. Certification emerged in the 1990s as the domain of less prestigious institutions with many faculty teaching on an adjunct basis after retirement from the public schools. As the professoriate changed, so did program emphasis and textbook adoption.

THE TEXTBOOKS

Listed below are the textbooks selected to represent the last part of the century. They are a far cry from compendiums of best practice of the common school era, but if one looks closely the heritage of the past is visible. With several exceptions they are smaller and less like general texts.

Carl Ashbaugh and Katherine L. Kasten. (1991). *Educational Leadership: Case Studies for Reflective Practice.*

Fenwick W. English. (1992). *Educational Administration: The Human Science.*

Reginald Green. (2000). *Practicing the Art of Leadership: A Problem-Based Approach to Implementing the ISLLC Standards.*

Emil Haller and Kenneth Strike. (1986). *An Introduction to Educational Administration: Social, Legal, and Ethical Perspectives.*

Wayne Hoy, Cecil Miskel, and Patrick Forsythe. (1996). *Educational Administration: Theory, Research, and Practice.* 5th ed.

John Hoyle, Fenwick English, and Betty Steffy. (1998). *Skills for Successful 21st Century School Leaders.*

Sherry Keith and Robert Girling. (1991). *Education, Management, and Participation: New Directions in Educational Administration.*

Theodore Kowalski and Ulrich Reitzug. (1993). *Contemporary School Administration: An Introduction.*

Fred Lunenburg and Allan Ornstein. (1996). *Educational Administration: Concepts and Practice.*

Katherine Merseth. (1997). *Case Studies in Educational Administration.*

M. K. Nee-Benham. (1999). *Case Studies for School Administrators.*

Robert Owens. (1995). *Organizational Behavior in Education.*

William Sharp, John Walters, and Helen Sharp. (2000). *Case Studies for School Leaders: Implementing the ISLLC Standards.*

Paula Short and Jay P. Scribner. (2000). *Case Studies for the Superintendency.*

Perhaps *Educational Administration: Theory, Practice, and Research* by Wayne Hoy, Cecil Miskel, and Patrick Forsythe (1996) illustrates the best of the late theory movement. It surveys a broad array of theorists both inside and outside the field of education. Its in-depth presentation of organization theory is undoubtedly the best in the textbook field. The book has long been criticized as a massive research review that does not always have application to educational organizations. Later editions have attempted to "public education base" the book, but it continues to live up to its reputation as a theory and research text. Terms such as the *superintendency* and the *principalship* seldom appear in the text body.

McGraw-Hill, publisher of its 1996 fifth edition, advertised it as the "heaviest revision to date," which is what generally happened to theory texts in this era. The company claimed that it was also the leading text in terms of sales.

Professors schooled in the theory movement may find Hoy, Miskel, and Forsythe's the best text to convey to master's level graduate students the important theoretical underpinnings of education. Other instructors might view the book as more appropriate for graduate students at the specialist or doctoral level who have already read a general introductory text.

The text best demonstrating a movement to a combination of theory, research, and practice is *Educational Administration: Concepts and Practices* (1996) by Fred Lunenburg and Allan Ornstein. In many editions (and perhaps many more to come) it reaches into the twenty-first century. The authors in the first eight chapters present the essentials of administrative theory, organization culture, human needs theory, and decision making. They competently cover content directly affecting the daily practice of administrators, such as building leadership, communication, governance, legal issues, instructional leadership, personnel supervision, and curriculum.

Lunenburg and Ornstein later complete a task often undertaken in the pretheory movement texts of providing introductory-level chapters on school governance and finance. This is usually very new information for most teachers. The specialized fields of school law and personnel give students an overview of these two important issue-laden areas.

The main interest of the book for students may be the later chapters on curriculum development and supervision so important to increasing teaching effectiveness. These closing chapters, just as those in governance, law, and finance, help students prepare for later specialized courses in law, finance, supervision, and instructional planning.

What makes this a very usable text is that it helps both the instructor and student to gain a broad overall picture of the profession. Each chapter ends with a section entitled "Administrative Advice," which assists students in implementing the text learnings. This helpful section in each chapter is a highlight of the text. The authors use pro-and-con debates to provoke both thought and discussion about content found in the chapters. Key terms, suggested readings, and discussion questions are included at the end of each chapter.

Lunenburg and Ornstein demonstrate that a text can present essential learning on theory and research and at the same time provide a solid and meaningful link to the day-to-day practice of school administration. It would be unfair to say they have watered down the massive array of research and theory found in Hoy and Miskel, but it is fair to say they have condensed the most important parts that best relate to the needs of an introductory-level graduate course.

Returning to the argument presented at the beginning of this chapter, I feel *Educational Administration: Concepts and Practice* heeds the cry of critics of educational-administration reform. It squarely focuses on the needs of the craft, rather than on demonstrating a scientific base for its practice.

The very interesting and readable text *Educational Administration: The Human Science* (1992), by Fenwick English, is a brief introduction. Interestingly, it is the first text reviewed that contains photographs. It gives students an excellent historical overview of school administration and public education. Management and governance theory is included, but not to the extent found in some other general texts. It does not provide a prelude to the specialized courses in school law and finance required by most programs. However, English ably ties together the present and the past, making it almost impossible for readers not to understand how schools and society have emerged and interface with each other.

Like Lunenberg and Ornstein, English writes directly to neophytes who are considering a career in educational administration. He poses questions to readers such as why they might consider the profession and then provides useful information about the requirements of being a school administrator. In the closing chapter he discusses with the reader what the literature says about the knowledge base and skills of exemplary practitioners. He sprinkles throughout the book suggestions for in-class activities.

Each chapter ends with an extensive list of references. In summary, *Educational Administration: The Human Science* is an adequate text, especially if supplemented by a case studies book. It is not as large and comprehensive as some other general texts. Unlike other texts reviewed, it spends a considerable amount of time portraying current life in schools and classrooms. English particularly emphasizes the importance culture has in the life of schools and what part administrators can play in making schools functional in a multicultural world. This text leans more to the foundation areas than other texts reviewed.

In summary, this text is different from other general textbooks in educational administration in that it is more tied to the daily world of everyday people and educators. It is historical, but current; brief, but complete in its treatment of essential theory; and useful for teachers thinking about a career in school administration. It is a very readable text.

The next textbook reviewed is *Education, Management and Participation* (1991) by Sherry Keith and Robert Girling. In some respects this is a miniature version of Lunenburg and Ornstein. Its organization is traditional with chapters in leadership, motivation, school community relations, finance, collective bargaining, and decision making. It is unique, however, in offering chapters on participative management and decision making. The reader will often wonder whether some of its chapters might be more appropriate in a specialized text discussing the principalship. In summary, this text is fairly well written, but so many of the topics are treated with such brevity that it does not furnish a knowledge base upon which the graduate student can move on to specialized courses in law, finance, and supervision.

The highlights of the text are the chapters that argue for participatory management. In these several chapters the authors advocate and describe participatory management, a current theme in many schools. During the era numerous school districts adopted site-based management and planning models.

Robert Owen's (1995) *Organizational Behavior in Education* is quite similar to Hoy and Miskel's text. It has been published in seven editions and is easily identifiable as a product of the theory movement. It moves somewhat beyond Hoy and Miskel in attempting to tie theory to practice. It, like other theory books, borrows theories and research from the behavioral and social sciences. It is perhaps the most readable of the theory texts. It also attempts to inform the reader of current interests and issues in education, such as gender awareness, diversity, multiculturalism, and standards for professional practice. This text, like Hoy and Miskel's, might be more appropriate for theory and management classes at the doctoral level.

Theodore Kowalski and Ulrich Reitzug's *Contemporary School Administration*, first published in 1993, discusses extensively the roles and behaviors of educational administrators. This is an excellent general text for use as an introduction to a graduate program focused on preparing practitioners. The two chapters on leadership vividly lay out the challenges of educational leadership and discuss leadership styles and behaviors in a very understandable manner. Each chapter ends with very helpful sections titled "Implications for Practice."

Unlike some of the other reviewed texts, Kowalski and Reitzug's book directly addresses school-reform issues and the role administrators might play in meeting demands to change or reform schools. Perhaps the strongest chapter in the text addresses the transformation of the school through the employment of planned change. A very perceptive chapter is also dedicated to the special role of women and minorities in educational administration.

Overall this is a strong and well-written text leaning a bit more toward practice than theory, but still classified as a dual-purpose text that works well in conjunction with a case studies text. Perhaps the most interesting thing about this text is that it is the last general textbook (without previous editions) written prior to 2000.

The last general-type text reviewed is *An Introduction to Educational Administration: Social, Legal and Ethical Perspectives* (1986) by Emil Haller and Kenneth Strike. The authors in the introduction notify the reader that their text is not like other general texts in educational administration.

The book format presents a case from real life at the beginning of each chapter and uses it as a lead-in to discussing a general topic or issue confronting practicing administrators. This was not an uncommon approach in the 1950s and 1960s for texts focusing on practice rather than theory. Moving past the introduction, the chapter organization seems to promise a text covering the basics of practice. This is not always accomplished in an easily understandable way.

Unfortunately, the authors do not choose their chapter topics or issues wisely. The lead-ins to cases are good, but chapters on issues such as crime, desegregation, discipline, student rights, and teacher evaluation might be left to more specialized texts. The core subject areas of leadership, organizational life, and management are too brief. This text does not compare favorably with the other general texts published between 1985 and 2000.

Perhaps the future of general texts is a focus on leadership. Leadership texts supported by casebooks may become dominant adoptions in the standards-driven era of twenty-first century reform. Professors may well use books such as *Skills for Successful 21st Century School Leaders: Standards for Peak Performers* (1998) to provide a standards focus for preparation. John Hoyle, Fenwick English, and Betty Steffy discuss the skills and performance levels required to manage and lead each major element of school operations, such as curriculum, instruction, staff development, and planning. This standards-based text can serve as an introduction to the field of educational administration. Some may call it a new era compendium of best practices based on the model of those produced by the grandfathers of the profession, Elwood Cubberley, George Strayer, and Jesse Sears.

Conceptually, *Skills for Successful 21st Century School Leaders* brings the theory movement full circle. A move toward practice is clearly discernable in this book at times reminiscent of the professional practice compendia. There is little doubt that the existence of large general texts will be challenged in future decades.

CASE STUDIES TEXTBOOKS

Many professors currently use a case studies textbook to supplement a general-type textbook, a fact that provides the rationale for reviewing them in this chapter. Very likely many instructors feel that the use of real-life cases in practice provides opportunities for students to fit theories and research into the real world of problem solving in schools. Many of the casebooks provide stimulating cases that students easily relate to from their viewpoints as teachers. A caution regarding case study books is that school issues and environments change, rendering many cases stale within a few years.

The first of the case study texts reviewed is *Educational Leadership: Case Studies for Reflective Practice* (1991) by Carl Ashbaugh and Katherine Kasten. The cases are grouped by categories: managing people, resources, politics and programs. The authors provide a brief overview of how students should analyze the case studies and translate learnings into practice. The cases are brief and focus on school, community, and district issues.

Theodore Kowalski's *Case Studies in Educational Administration* (1995) provides a series of cases about problems in both schools and districts. He introduces each case with background and identifies the problem of the case. Following the case presentation, he provides questions for reflection and key issues to consider. He also provides the reader and instructor with a listing of what key theories and themes are present in each case. This is a very good usable casebook in its third edition. It is a good fit with most of the general-type texts. It is likely the most popular of the casebook texts.

A third casebook is *Case Studies in Educational Administration* (1997) by Katherine Merseth. This case study text provides an excellent guide for students using casebooks to study six important areas of educational administration. This casebook is also a most appropriate companion for general texts like Lunenberg and Ornstein.

A casebook not focusing on specific standards is *Case Studies for School Administrators* (1999) by M. K. P. Nee-Benham. Of the casebooks it provides the best description of how case studies are scientifically structured and developed. It also presents a set of protocols to use in solving the cases in practice. Interestingly, the cases are clearly based on prominent theories of leadership and organizational change. This is probably the most scholarly of the casebooks reviewed.

Several casebooks focus on the ISLLC standards that serve as the basis of certification in about thirty states. The most ambitious of these casebooks is *Case Studies for School Leaders* (2001) by William Sharp, James Walters, and Helen Sharp. A surprising 138 cases are presented, along with the requisite standards and performance objectives. Discussion questions follow each of the cases.

Another ISLLC-based textbook is *Practicing the Art of Leadership: A Problem-Based Approach to Implementing the ISLLC Standards* (2000) by Reginald Green. It contains fewer cases with a closer focus on the problems of practice, at the same time addressing ISLLC standards. This casebook, like the others focused on the ISLLC standards, aims, it seems, to be not a supplement, but a stand-alone text. This might be appropriate in the case of a field-based class that is part of an administrative internship.

All of the reviewed casebooks focus primarily on the practice of principals with the exception of Paula Short and Jay Pardes Scribner's edited book, *Case Studies of the Superintendency* (2000), which presents ten case studies by various authors focusing on the day-to-day problems superintendents face. Questions and suggested learning activities follow each case. The focus of this casebook on the superintendency is timely as very little textbook literature exists for the preparation of superintendents. In the general-textbook arena, only two true examples are in print.

A significant problem with casebooks is that they are casebooks. While providing a very helpful tool to assist students in putting theory and research into practice, they fall short as stand-alone texts. It seems the mission of a general text is to provide an introduction and broad overview introducing students to a profession. Casebooks are snapshots of pieces of that profession.

EDUCATIONAL ADMINISTRATION
TEXTBOOK PUBLISHERS

Most, if not all, general textbooks in educational administration are printed by large publishers. Until recently a few publishers have dominated the market. I wonder if editors have significant influence in determining the content of these texts. If so, perhaps the need for sales revenue is influencing the field. Smaller publishers such as Scarecrow (Technomic), Sage, Corwin, and Longman typically have not ventured into the large hardcover general-textbook market. They have been active in getting casebooks on the market and have always provided an outlet for specialized educational-administration books.

It is legitmate to ask whether publishers pass on to prospective authors their opinions as to what will outsell the competition. This is especially so with general texts going through multiple editions and updates. The new material added seems in some cases to be the result of editors' efforts to insure that the new edition contains the new "isms" in vogue (and marketable) at the time. First editions are generally well reviewed and critiqued by educational-administration professors and practitioners. Later editions likely are intensely "field reviewed."

Certainly publishers must be sensitive to what the current trends might be in the field. And they cannot get caught publishing new editions that gain few course adoptions. The split camps in educational administration make this difficult. The first camp comprises the professors schooled in the theory movement and holds that just-admitted graduate students cannot understand the profession and its practice without first understanding the theory and research. The first task for this group of professors is to teach theory. The second camp of professors feels that problems of practice can be introduced along with theory from the outset of a student's training. A good example of this professorial dualism can be seen in adoptions of Hoy and Miskel and perhaps Lunenburg and Ornstein.

It is unlikely that the theory versus practice controversy will ever abate. In the future, general texts (if there are any) will be dual texts focusing on professional history, societal foundations, leadership, motivation, communication, decision making, and supervision.

It appears that textbooks in the twenty-first century will be affected by the current trend toward preparation standards. ISLLC standards and indicators of performance have been adopted as licensure criteria by over thirty states. The question naturally arises whether any forthcoming general texts will be organized around these standards. Will nonvalidated standards rather than research or theory drive the next generation of texts? Lastly, with the growth in casebooks, standards books, hot topic books, and specialty books, the future for the general textbook seems uncertain.

REFERENCES

Ashbaugh, C. R., and Kasten, L. (1991). *Educational leadership: case studies for reflective practice.* New York: Longman.

Berliner, D. C., and Biddle, B. J. (1995). *The manufactured crisis: myths, fraud, and the attack on America's public schools.* Boston: Addison-Wesley.

Chub, J. E., and Moe, T. (1990). *Politics, markets, and America's schools.* Washington, D.C.: Brookings Institution.

Conley, D. T. (1993). *Roadmap to reform.* Eugene: ERIC.

Culbertson, J. A. (1988). A century's quest for a knowledge base. In Boylan, N. (ed.). *Handbook on research on educational administration.* New York: Longman, pp. 3–26.

English, F. W. (1992). *Educational administration: the human science.* New York: Harper-Collins.

Glass, T. E., Bjork, L., and Brunner, C. (2000). *The study of the American school superintendency: 2000.* Arlington: American Association of School Administrators.

Green, R. L. (2000). *Practicing the art of leadership: a problem-based approach to implementing the ISLLC standards.* Upper Saddle River: Prentice Hall.

Griffiths, D. E. (1988). Reform PDQ or RIP. Invited address, Division A, American Educational Research Association, New Orleans, April 14.

Haller, E. J., and Strike, K. A. (1986). *An introduction to educational administration: social, legal, and ethical perspectives.* New York: Longman.

Hanushek, E. A. (1994). *Making schools work: improving performance and controlling costs.* Washington, D.C.: Brookings Institution.

Hoy, W. K., Miskel, C., and Forsythe, P. (1996). *Educational administration: theory, research, and practice.* 5th ed. New York: McGraw-Hill.

Hoyle, J. R., English, F. W., and Steffy, B. E. (1998). *Skills for successful 21st century school leaders: standards for peak performance.* 2nd ed. Arlington: American Association of School Administrators.

Keith, S., and Girling, R. (1991). *Education, management, and participation: new directions in educational administration.* Boston: Allyn and Bacon.

Kowalski, T. J. (1995). *Case studies in educational administration.* 2nd ed. New York: Longman.

Kowalski, T. J., and Reitzug, U. C. (1993). *Contemporary school administration: an introduction.* New York: Longman.

Lunenburg, F. C., and Ornstein, A. C. (1996). *Educational administration: concepts and practice.* 2nd ed. Belmont: Wadsworth.

McCarthy, M., and Kuh, G. (1997). *Continuity and change: the educational leadership professoriate.* Columbia: University Council on School Administration.

Merseth, K. K. (1997). *Case studies in educational administration.* New York: Longman.

National Commission on Excellence in Education. (1983). *A nation at risk: the imperative for educational reform.* Washington, D.C.: USDOE.

National Policy Board for Educational Administration. (1989). *Improving the preparation of school administrators: An agenda for reform.* Charlottesville: Author.

Nee-Benham, M. K. P. (1999). *Case studies for school administrators.* Lancaster: Technomic.

Owens, R. G. (1995). *Organizational behavior in education.* 4th ed. Boston: Allyn and Bacon.

Sarason, S. B. (1990). *The predictable failure of educational reform.* San Francisco: Jossey-Bass.

Sharp, W. L., Walters, J. K., and Sharp, H. M. (2001). *Case studies for school leaders: implementing the ISLLC standards.* Lanham: Scarecrow.

Short, P. M., and Scribner, J. P. (2000). *Case studies of the superintendency.* Lanham: Scarecrow.

Sizer, T. R. (1992). *Horace's school: redesigning the American high school.* Boston: Houghton-Mifflin.

Tyack, D., and Cuban, L. (1995). *Tinkering toward utopia: a century of public school reform.* Cambridge: Harvard University Press.

8

An Overview: School-Administration
Texts, 1820–2000

Thomas E. Glass

It is difficult to identify the first textbook in educational administration. In the nineteenth century school teaching and school administering were often one and the same thing. The era of common schools, discussed in chapter 2, begins a journey through the text literature by setting the birth date for the profession at 1820. Prior to that time, head teachers supervised schools without assistance from intermediary professional school administrators. Early American popular literature often stereotypes the schoolmaster as providing necessary supervision (and the rod) to recalcitrant students. In return, local board members closely supervised the schoolmaster. The role of school administrator did not really exist outside the largest school systems until the turn of the century when the little red schoolhouse faded into obscurity.

Perhaps the dominant theme in American education during the nineteenth century was the ascendancy of the common school. Since the first settlements religious dogma and churches had dominated education. In fact, education was religious education and the curriculum reflected that one needed to be a good Protestant. Horace Mann and other common school disciples began a quasi-religious movement in the 1840s that soon spread across most of the nation. Perhaps the literature best chronicling the movement is *Managers of Virtue: Public School Leadership in America, 1920–1980* (1982) by David Tyack and Elisabeth Hansot. They provide probably the best overview of the development of American school and its leadership.

Many early education authors like Samuel Dutton and William Payne were interested not in history, but in providing schoolmasters and perhaps lay board members with guidelines to school keeping. This was contained in numerous how-to manuals long on advice, short on theory and fact. In addition, the early authors were almost obsessively concerned with promoting and maintaining the strict moral upbringing required by the Anglo-Saxon Protestant work ethic that was so much a part of life in the America of their time (Tyack and Hansot, 1982, pp. 7–10).

As might be expected, schools and school management by the turn of the twentieth century reflected evidence of growing urbanism. Cities such as New York, Chicago, Boston, Philadelphia, Detroit, and Cleveland suddenly found themselves with immense school systems costing taxpayers millions of dollars to operate. Along with the explosion in the number of school buildings was a pressing need for some type of centralized cost-efficient organizational model. This was a major impetus in development of the position titled "general superintendent of schools."

The management of a school district by one person did not occur suddenly or without conflict. The management of large school districts for many years was the domain of two people, the superintendent and the business manager, each selected independently of the other by the elected or appointed school board. Samuel Dutton and David Snedden in *The Administration of Public Education in the United States* (1908) provide a glimpse of these times by picturing the superintendent as being a moral leader and a protector of what is virtuous in the community. The business manager was entrusted for the proper husbandry of important district finances (Dutton, 1909, pp. 3–10). This is not to say Dutton and Snedden agreed with the dual-leadership system.

Dutton, probably the leading author of texts, by 1903 had produced an extensive compendium of order, strictness, and the day-to-day routine of running a school or district. Another representative of the pre–World War I period's influence on administrative texts is William Chancellor, who most decidedly tells the nation's schoolmasters what is and is not moral and what should be done away with in order to save the souls of students. To Chancellor's credit, he foretells the beginnings of the child-centered school and a philosophy to later flower under John Dewey. In brief, the period between 1820 and 1914 was one where order and morals were strongly emphasized in a relentless number of pages. Very little theory and science followed the common school movement.

Religion was the theme of the day, with a dash of common sense, order, and procedure. In general, the texts reviewed in chapter 2 of this book capture the common school movement and contemporary society. Whether or not these textbooks were significant influences in the development of the school district concept is debatable. It would seem they must have had a degree of influence on the school leadership of the day. Schoolmasters had few precedents to fall back upon in developing the new educational system.

This chapter raises a most important question: have the general texts influenced the development of the profession and schools, or have contemporary social and intellectual forces influenced the texts? Or has there been a simultaneous mixture of the two? For the period of 1820 to 1914, my guess would be that the latter was occurring, especially after the turn of the century.

The onset of World War I brought many changes to American society, including a need for better educational systems to serve the growing middle class. The needs of industry, business, and the professions in an age of developing technology called for substantial changes in school curriculum and management.

Textbooks in education became more specialized, including those prescribing the management of schools. One of the most interesting education books in of the time was published before the war and in many subsequent editions. Paul Monroe's *Cyclopaedia of Education* (1911) provided the reader with just about everything educators needed to know about education. Monroe mentions that in 1910, 348 book titles existed in the field of education, with more than several in educational administration. Importantly, the texts of the period called for empirical knowledge as the basis of managing schools and school programs. Perhaps this was a subtle movement to remove religion from the schools. Surely, the profession was in the process of being professionalized. The texts of the day do denote a decline in moral teaching and emphasis on religious values.

The creation of departments of educational administration in higher-education institutions contributed to a movement establishing a practice base for administration in the twentieth century. Many students in these early departments, with their professors as mentors, later gained superintendent positions in urban districts across the nation. They furnished the first cadre to practice the empirically oriented wisdom learned in higher-education courses (Tyack and Hansot, 1982, pp. 130–135).

In addition to an increasing number of book titles originating at Teachers College, Stanford University, the University of Chicago, and New York University, national associations like the NEA sponsored research and publication funding opportunities for writers and professors in educational administration. There is little doubt that the NEA is the parent organization of the field of educational administration.

The works of George Strayer and Robert Thorndike of Teachers College represent the prevailing emphasis of the period on factual administration. Thorndike's "connectionism" and Strayer's "financial surveys" were seminal to the developments in educational administration during the period. Despite the prolific output of these two authors, Ellwood Cubberley of Stanford was the period's dominant author. Many of Thorndike's and Strayer's books can be classified as scholarly works not entirely suitable for use as general texts. Not so for Cubberley, as he moved from *Changing Conceptions* of *Education* (1909) to a broad range of titles, before concluding in 1934 with a book of readings. It is an understatement to say that Cubberley influenced several generations of students in general administration classes around the nation. He is descriptive and assuredly authoritative (Cubberley, 1934). His books were readable and set the tone of educational-administration programs in numerous institutions across the country. Cubberley is often called the grandfather of the educational-administration professoriate.

Textbooks originating in university programs and authored by professors and occasionally superintendents in the field were probably very influential on how schools were administered and districts were governed. The prolific output of empiricists such as Strayer and Thorndike produced hundreds of thousands of statistics used to direct administrators in how to perform daily management tasks. Scientific management became supreme in the large urban districts during this period of rapid urban growth (Callahan, 1962). Management science, at the time, was the scientific management of Frederick Taylor and had a significant impact on the thought of professors, graduate students, and superintendents.

A last note describing the period was mentoring by university professors. High-profile professors such as Elliot, Cubberley, and Strayer were notorious for placing their students in leading superintendencies. This system is well documented in *Managers of Virtue* and, probably more than anything else, insured the influence of textbooks written by sponsoring professors. This also firmly tied together the careers of the professors and superintendents. This mentoring existed in regional universities, but more so with principals than superintendents (Tyack and Hansot, 1982, pp. 133–134).

Despite the Great Depression, a clear conceptual theme emerges in the 1934–1945-period textbook literature. The struggle between the dualism of the conventional wisdom of the past and emerging concepts of the role of the school in society raged in classrooms and at professional conferences. This was a question of choice between maintaining the society of the past through the schooling enterprise or changing society by using education as the change agent.

During this period, a considerable number of field-based research projects were conducted, examining nearly every management function. Classroom sizes, physical space arrangements, curriculum organization, teacher certification, and teacher training were among the many tasks studied. Later, the professors conducting the studies transferred the data into general textbooks. In brief, the early professors planted seeds and reaped young professors who continued the academic work of their mentors.

Noteworthy is the appearance of textbooks in specialized areas of administration such as finance. However, the general trend of textbooks containing vast amounts of conventional wisdom obtained from surveys and good practice continued to dominate the titles in an expanding graduate educational-administration market. Administration was growing in both numbers of administrators and their special roles, which were made necessary by scientific-management principles.

The Great Depression furnished a stage for a reexamination of the basic purposes of education. Humanists like John Dewey, William Kilpatrick, and George S. Counts questioned the very foundations of American society as held together by the public schools (Tyack, Lowe, and Hansot, 1984). The human condition during the Depression had shocked many academics, especially those in educational philosophy. The back of the previous "god" of scientific management, with its accompanying emphasis on technology and production, had been broken by Black Friday on the New York Stock Exchange. If education was not to be carried out on a quasi-corporate production model, what path should it take? What was to be the future role or mission of the schools? Texts began to emerge in the mid-1930s that gave a hint. In *Educational Administration As Social Policy* (1934), Jesse Newlon states the four basic purposes of schools should be (1) transmission of the culture, (2) education for citizenship, (3) social control, and (4) vocational efficiency. Newlon went on to say that education had always been focused on a static society, instead of merging and emerging purposes and needs (Callahan, 1962, pp. 200–203).

Thus, the first group of social reformist writers of the educational world began to influence the textbook literature in most areas of the profession. This type of critical theory was to become quite commonplace over the next forty years, cresting in the reform-dominated 1960s and early 1970s. Many times the reformists attempted general textbooks with the purpose of overturning all of the old themes and platitudes of desired and good principles of educational administration; however, their attempts rarely if ever survived more than a first printing and limited distribution.

Simply put, most professors of educational administration were former schoolmen in that static society and in no way could be seen as social or political reformers of a liberal persuasion. This has been the case throughout educational-administration history. Professors of educational administration have been in their institutions leaders in the preservation of the historical purpose of higher education in America, namely, the maintainance of the status quo.

Again, in the 1940s many educational-administration text writers called for a reformulation of the purposes of public education. However, they did not advocate revolution or radical reform. Instead, they asked institutions to modify philosophical orientations from strict authoritarianism to democratic cooperation between teachers and administrators. A democratic theme of shared governance emerges time and again.

Returning to the dualism problem mentioned earlier, the field of texts had been and was still dominated by works containing many chapters about buildings, playgrounds, personnel records, schedules, and all of the internal management tasks associated with running a school. Average practice in the average school and school district was the modus operandi. Seldom do the general-text authors discuss the purpose to which administrators are to administrate the schools: "Don't think about it, do it" is the prescription outlined in the standard five-hundred-page books of the day.

A few authors bring up the sticky problem of purpose in their first chapters. *Democracy in School Administration* (1943) by Koopman, Miel, and Misner is the bell ringer of this group. The influence of Dewey can be seen in their view of the individual and society (Koopman, Miel, and Misner, 1943, p. v). By the end of this period, traditional writers no longer thought of schools as isolated bastions of learning and the moral teachings necessary for virtue. The impact of the expanding fields of sociology, anthropology, political science, and psychology were beginning to have what would soon be a substantial impact on education.

After World War II, textbook writers again returned to the themes of the social processes of the school coupled with the principles of good administrative practice. The nation as well as public education was interested in just what the result of twelve years of formal schooling was to be. Due to the tremendous social upheaval caused by World War II, democracy emerged as a dominant theme. It was important to emphasize, hold onto, and increase what was democratic and "American" in order to keep America safe for democracy. A cornerstone of democracy was the local community, and during this period writers such as Paul Mort and Jesse Sears did much to promote the goodness of the school in meeting identified needs of the community and, perhaps more importantly, promoted the desirability of the local school board.

The local board was the true and best representative of the people in a democracy funding schools for all regardless of race, religion, creed, or national origin. Text after text dedicated chapters to arguing for the adoption of democratic philosophies by every district with administrators and boards in leadership roles.

Then, text writers enter into discussions of the intricacies of each administrative function to be performed. Expert advice is given on the specific, along with expert principles grounded on best practices discovered in solid empirical studies of past years by the intellectual godfathers of educational administration. The textbooks during this era perhaps more than in any other reflect the social and political turmoil of the time. They strive for direction based on common sense, patriotism, structure, and stability. In many, there is a feeling that education is embarking on a fearful voyage into a new world.

The path to a new future emerges in the mid-1950s as authors Daniel Griffiths and Andrew Halpin advocate the development of an administrative theory in opposition to the factualism of the past. As the numbers of professors of administration dramatically increased after the war, so did the numbers of sociologists and psychologists developing social and behavioral science theory. By the mid-1960s, organizational theory chapters begin to appear in some general texts. In 1968, a text authored by Jacob Getzels, James Lipham, and Roald Campbell became the first theory text to totally discard factualism. It strongly emphasized theory and directly borrowed from the social and behavioral sciences. It definitely took textbooks in a new direction, what Halpin (1966) would later refer to as the new movement.

This did not mean scientific management and factualism was dead and buried. General texts continued to appear containing large amounts of descriptive material and expert opinion. The principles survived despite emergence of the new theory. The new movement has not been totally successful in displacing descriptive studies. Both have their respective value to the profession. Interestingly, both have improved over the past several decades, becoming more scholarly. Today they present a dilemma, as most instructors can see a need for what each offers, but cannot adopt both as a course text. What did not emerge during the 1960s and 1970s was a good multivolume super text providing descriptive or theoretical research supported by theory.

The textbook period between 1985 and 2000 was one of intense school reform. The release of *A Nation at Risk* in 1983 launched public schools on a politically motivated crusade of top-down reform. State after state passed legislation to reform schools. The first targets in the path of reformists were classroom teachers. Later, in the 1990s, school leadership was targeted. Traditional school administration was seen by reformists to be a large part of the problem. Instructional leadership was thought to be the key to academic improvement. In fact, the traditional theme of developing well-rounded students to become productive citizens in a democratic society was left out of reform discussions. By the 1990s thousands of academic standards were put in place by legislation, and test scores became the dominant determinant for curriculum and instruction.

Textbook literature during this period became reform literature. Publishers challenged by massive consolidation in the publishing industry began to publish books that promised to be hot and quick sells. General textbooks in educational administration were seen as profitable only if they were published in multiple editions. I was unable to find a completely new general text in educational administration written in its first edition after 1993. Some texts in 2003 were in their seventh and eighth editions. Chapters on reform, gender issues, multiculturalism, and accountability have been added to many of the texts to keep them current and marketable.

The professorate changed during the last two decades of the twentieth century. Currently, according to the University Council on Educational Administration, fewer than half of educational-administration professors have been practicing school administrators. This may well account for the dearth of new general textbooks in educational administration. The professors simply have neither the breadth of experience nor the preparation to write such works. In general, their professional training has been narrow, and it should be expected they would be more interested in writing texts around a specialty such as law, policy, finance, or instructional leadership.

Interestingly, many of the general texts of the 1990s are attempts to marry theory with research and practice. And many casebooks emerged during this period to provide students with opportunities to use theory in classroom simulations. These casebooks bring practice closer to theory and seem to be the future of textbook publishing, along with specialized texts to accompany licensing standards. The message is that if it is not covered in a standard, it is not part of administering schools and districts. There is little doubt that reductionism and micro theory may be the dominant themes for twenty-first century educational-administration literature.

SUMMARY OF TEXTBOOK ERAS

School Administration Is Born: 1820–1914

Every profession must grow through a series of developmental stages from birth to maturity. This has been the case with educational administration growing alongside the common school movement. As the numbers of schools increased, so did the need for administrators. The increase later produced a need for multischool organizations known as districts. The role of administrators at first was to act as the guardians and teachers of morals and ethics held by Protestant America. Lay governance boards strictly controlled the actions and practice of early administrators. Administrators were trained to model the behavior of other administrators. Apprenticeship was informal and state certification began to emerge slowly during this era.

The dominant theme of this early textbook literature is the "cookbook" approach. As there were few colleges of education, the books were written so that a "man" could stay at home and read how to be an administrator in front of "his" hearth. The early texts strongly reflected Protestant themes, and prayer in school was common. Also common were the practices thought best to manage schools. Lastly, good leaders were those who possessed a common set of traits found in "successful" leaders in "successful" schools. The following were the leading texts of this era:

William E. Chancellor. (1915). *Our Schools: Their Administration and Supervision.*

William E. Chancellor. (1907). *A Theory of Motives, Ideals, and Values in Education.* Boston: Houghton Mifflin.

Samuel T. Dutton. (1909). *School Management.* Rev. 1903 ed.

Samuel T. Dutton and David Snedden. (1908). *The Administration of Public Education in the United States.*

Samuel R. Hall. (1829). *Lectures on School-Keeping.*

Samuel R. Hall. (1832). *Lectures to Female Teachers on School-Keeping.*

National Education Association. (1895). *Journal of Proceedings and Addresses*, pp. 375–397.

David P. Page. (1885). *Theory and Practice of Teaching* (originally published in 1847; new edition, edited and enlarged by W. H. Payne).

William H. Payne. (1875). *Chapters on School Supervision.*

William H. Payne. (1901). *Education of Teachers.*

Preston W. Search. (1901). *An Ideal School.*

The Contemporary Science Period: 1915–1933

Education or school administration had become a profession by the beginning of World War I. Specialization in administration had begun to develop and would carry the tenets of scientific management into every school and classroom. The emphasis on specialization and efficiency accompanied a rapid growth in the numbers of schools and districts. Urban districts served as lighthouses in administrative practice. A sweeping surge of empiricism in educational administration occurred in numerous large city school surveys conducted by the "fathers of the profession." The mass of data generated by the studies identified efficient practices of administration. The opinions of experts in some cases became the law of educational administration.

There was a decided effort on the part of the newly professionalized superintendents in the large districts to use scientific-management principles to discourage intrusion by lay boards into management. Truly, the profession of educational administration was born and recognized. The following were the leading textbooks of the era:

John C. Almack and James F. Bursch. (1925). *The Administration of Consolidated and Village Schools.*

Fred C. Ayer and A. S. Barr. (1928). *The Organization of Supervision.*

Ina G. Barnes. (1929). *Rural School Management.*

Mabel Carney. (1912). *Country Life and the Country School.*

William E. Chancellor. (1904). *Our Schools: Their Administration and Supervision.*

Ellwood P. Cubberley. (1916). *Public School Administration.*

Ellwood P. Cubberley. (1927). *State School Administration: A Textbook of Principles.*

Horace M. Culter and Julia M. Stone. (1913). *The Rural School: Its Methods and Management.*

Paul Hanus. (1913). *School Efficiency: A Constructive Study Applied to New York City.*

Paul Hanus. (1920). *School Administration and School Reports.*

William M. Maxwell. (1912). *A Quarter Century of Public School Development.*

Paul Monroe (ed.). (1911). *A Cyclopaedia of Education.*

Jessee B. Sears. (1925). *The School Survey: A Textbook on the Use of School Surveying in the Administration of Public Schools.*

George D. Strayer and Edward L. Thorndike. (1913). *Educational Administration: Quantitative Studies.*

George D. Strayer and N. L. Engelhardt. (1925). *Problems in Educational Administration.*

Oscar Weber. (1930). *Problems in Public School Administration.*

Common Sense to Concepts: 1934–1945

The Great Depression created an upheaval in America felt in education and reflected in the textbooks on administration. The almost total belief in scientific management came to be questioned by a new group of humanists. Textbooks began to ask administrators what the role of the school should be in a democratic society. What was the goal for children? Commonsense principles were insufficient for many text writers of this period. Managing schools to develop and shape the society became an increasingly heard theme. The words "cooperation," "participation," and "democracy" appear throughout the period, as writers responded to the teaching of John Dewey and George Counts. What might be the purpose of a school in the society of tomorrow? Perhaps this period is best characterized as one of self-examination. The following were leading texts of the Depression era:

Edwin J. Brown. (1938). *Secondary School Administration.*
Walter D. Cocking and Kenneth R. Williams. (1940). *The Education of School Administrators.*
Newton Edwards and Herman Richey. (1947). *The School in the American Social Order.*
Richard E. Jaggers. (1934). *Administering the County School System.*
Robert G. Koopman, Alice Miel, and Paul J. Misner. (1943). *Democracy in School Administration.*
Leonard Koos et al. (1940). *Administering the Secondary School.*
Jessee H. Newlon. (1934). *Educational Administration As Social Policy.*
William C. Reavis. (1939). *Democratic Practices in School Administration.*
William C. Reavis. (1941). *Administrative Adjustments Required by Socio-Economic Change.*
Samuel E. Weber. (1937). *Cooperative Administration and Supervision of the Teaching Personnel.*
Ernest C. Witham. (1936). *Problem Studies in School Administration.*

An Era of Propaganda and Rhetoric: 1946–1953

The dominant themes in the texts of this brief period were democracy and community. Democracy prevailed as a goal after the turmoil caused in society by World War II. This era itself was turbulent as McCarthyism vied with liberalism to chart the course of American life. The schools were simultaneously advocating democracy in classrooms and social liberalism. Communities still expected them to be traditional and practical. Most students still entered the work force after high school.

Many textbooks during this period emphasize the importance of community and the local school board. The writers of the time perceive a changing America, but really do not know where it is going or whether they wish to shape its direction. As the number of administrators being trained increased, the textbook literature became a somewhat confused blend of commonsense principles, scientific management, democracy, and human relations.

Texts from this period give very little indication that an academic revolution was in the wings. The following were lead texts of the postwar era:

Willard Elsbree and Harold McNally. (1951). *Elementary School Administration and Supervision.*

James H. Fox. (1949). *School Administration: Principles and Procedures.*

Harlan Hagman. (1951). *The Administration of American Public Schools.*

Albert Huggett. (1950). *Practical School Administration.*

Arthur Moehlman. (1951). *School Administration.*

Paul R. Mort. (1946). *Principles of School Administration: A Synthesis of Basic Concepts.*

Benjamin Pittinger. (1951). *Local Public School Administration.*

Ward J. Reeder (1939). *The Administration of Pupil Transportation.*

Jesse B. Sears. (1947). *Public School Administration.*

Jesse B. Sears. (1950). *The Nature of the Administrative Process.*

William Yauch. (1949). *Improving Human Relations in School Administration.*

Factualism to Theory to Science: 1955–1985

The prevailing themes of this period are the development of administrative theory and the use of research, theory, and methodology in administering schools. The first years saw the struggle for the development and acceptance of administrative theory. Applications of social and behavioral science research and tools were a second dominant theme. The period is generally perceived to be an era of the ascendance and dominance of the social sciences in educational administration. This is not reflected in the general types of texts. Many general texts were written and rewritten to remain descriptive tomes of expert opinion and administrative practice. The following were the leading texts of the period:

Roald F. Campbell, George Madsen, and Joseph Kinchloe. (1985). *Organization and Control of American Schools*. 5th ed.

Fred D. Carver and Thomas Sergiovanni. (1973). *The New School Executive: A Theory of Administration.*

Jacob Getzels, James Lipham, and Roald Campbell. (1968). *Educational Administration As Social Process.*

Calvin Grieder, Thomas Pierce, and E. Forbis Jordan. (1961). *Public School Administration*. 3rd ed.

Mark Hanson. (1979). *Educational Administration and Organizational Behavior.*

Ralph Kimbrough and Michael Nunnery. (1976). *Educational Administration: An Introduction.*

Steven Knezevich. (1984). *Administration of Public Education*. 4th ed.

Van Miller, George Madden, and Joseph Kinchloe. (1972). *The Public Administration of American School Systems*. 3rd ed.

William Monahan (ed.). (1975). *Theoretical Dimensions of Educational Administration.*

Edgar Morphet et al. (1984). *Educational Organizations and Administration*. 4th ed.

Clarence Newell (1978). *Human Behavior in Educational Administration.*

A Retreat from Theory in an Era of Reform: 1985–2000

This period of literature is dominated by school-reform efforts beginning in 1983. Many general textbooks written in the previous era continued on into new editions. Some were slanted toward the theory movement, and others combined both theory and practice. Of special interest in this period is the appearance of case studies texts, specialized texts, and texts written to help graduate students and practitioners meet new professional standards.

The general textbook began to fade out during this era. Only one completely new general text was published. Textbooks in this period illustrate the tension caused by reform. They also illustrate the dissolution of the academic field of educational administration into many splinter groups. The following are among the leading texts of the period:

Carl R. Ashbaugh and Katherine Kasten. (1991). *Educational Leadership: Case Studies for Reflective Practice.*

Fenwick English. (1992). *Educational Administration: The Human Science.*

Reginald L. Green. (2000). *Practicing the Art of Leadership: A Problem-Based Approach to Implementing the ISLLC Standards.*

Emil Haller and Kenneth Strike. (1986). *An Introduction to Educational Administration: Social, Legal, and Ethical Perspectives.*

Wayne Hoy, Cecil Miskel, and Patrick Forsythe. (1996). *Educational Administration: Theory, Research, and Practice.* 5th ed.

John Hoyle, Fenwick English, and Betty Steffy. (1998). *Skills for Successful 21st Century School Leaders: Standards for Peak Performance.*

Sherry Keith and Robert Girling. (1991). *Education, Management, and Participation: New Directions in Educational Administration.*

Theodore Kowalski and Ulrich Reitzug. (1993). *Contemporary School Administration: An Introduction.*

Theodore Kowalski. (1995). *Case Studies in Educational Administration.*

Fred C. Lunenburg and Allan Ornstein. (1996). *Educational Administration: Concepts and Practice.* 2nd ed.

Katherine Merseth. (1997). *Case Studies in Educational Administration.*

M. K. P. Nee-Benham. (1999). *Case Studies for School Administrators.*

Robert Owens. (1995). *Organizational Behavior in Education.* 4th ed.

William Sharp, James Walters, and Helen Sharp. (2001). *Case Studies for School Leaders: Implementing the ISLLC Standards.*

Paula Short and Jay P. Scribner. (2000). *Case Studies for the Superintendency.*

REFERENCES

Callahan, R. E. (1962). *Education and the cult of efficiency.* Chicago: The University of Chicago Press.

Cubberley, E. P. (1934). *Readings in public education in the United States.* Boston: Houghton Mifflin.

Dutton, S. T. (1909). *School management.* Rev. 1903 ed. New York: Scribner's.

Getzels, J., Lipham, J., and Campbell, R. F. (1968). *Educational administration as social process.* New York: Harper and Row.

Halpin, A. (1966). *Theory and research in administration.* New York: Macmillan.

Koopman, G., Miel, A., and Misner, P. (1943). *Democracy in school administration.* New York: Appleton-Century-Crofts.

Monroe, P. (ed.). (1911). *A cyclopaedia of education.* New York: Macmillan.

Tyack, D. B., and Hansot, E. (1982). *Managers of virtue: public school leadership in America, 1820–1980.* New York: Basic Books.

Tyack, D. B., Lowe, R., and Hansot, E. (1984). *Public schools in hard times.* Cambridge: Harvard University Press.

References

Adams, H. P., and Dickey, F. G. (1953). *Basic principles of supervision.* New York: American Book Co.

Almack, J. C., and Bursch, J. F. (1925). *The administration of consolidated and village schools.* Boston: Houghton Mifflin.

American Association of School Administrators (AASA). (1947). *Schools for a new world. Twenty-fifth yearbook of the AASA.* Washington, D.C.: Author.

AASA. (1955). *Staff relations in school administration. Thirty-third yearbook of the AASA.* Washington, D.C.: Author.

Annual report of the school committee of Boston. (1859). Boston: Author.

Asbaugh, C. R., and Kasten, L. (1991). *Educational leadership: case studies for reflective practice.* White Plains: Longman.

Ayer, F. C., and Barr, A. S. (1928). *The organization of supervision.* New York: Appleton.

Barnes, I. G. (1929). *Rural school management.* New York: Macmillan.

Bartky, J. A. (1953). *Supervision as human relations.* Boston: Heath.

Benjamin, H. (1942). *Emergent conceptions of the school administrator's task* (Cubberley lecture of November 12, 1938, at the Stanford School of Education). Stanford, Calif.: Stanford University Press.

Berliner, D. C., and Biddle, B. J. (1995). *The manufactured crisis.* Reading: Addison-Wesley.

Boardman, C. W., Douglas, H. R., and Bent, Rudyard K. (1953). *Democratic supervision in secondary schools.* Boston: Houghton Mifflin.

Briggs, T. H. (1952). *Improving instruction through supervision.* New York: Macmillan.

Brown, E. J. (1938). *Secondary school administration.* Boston: Houghton Mifflin.

Brubacher, J. S. (1966). *A history of the problems of education.* New York: McGraw-Hill.

Butterworth, J. E. (1926). *Principles of rural school administration.* New York: Macmillan.

Butterworth, J. E., and Ruegsegger, V. (1941). *Administering pupil transportation.* Minneapolis: Educational Publishers.

Butts, F. R. (1955). *A cultural history of western education.* New York: McGraw-Hill.

Callahan, R. E. (1964). *Changing conceptions of the superintendency in public education, 1865–1964.* Cambridge: New England School Development Council.

Callahan, R. E. (1962). *Education and the cult of efficiency.* Chicago: University of Chicago Press.

Campbell, C. M. (1952). *Practical applications of democratic administration.* New York: Harper.

Campbell, R. F. (1959). Peculiarities in educational administration. In Halpin A. (ed.). *Administrative theory in education.* New York: Macmillan, p. 71.

Campbell, R. F. (1972). Educational administration: a twenty-five year perspective. *Educational Administration Quarterly* 8 (Spring): 1–25.

Campbell, R. F., Madden, G., and Kinchelow, J. R. (1985). *Organization and control of American schools.* 5th ed. Columbus: Merrill.

Campbell, R. F., and Gregg, R. T. (eds.). (1957). *Administrative behavior in education.* New York: Harper and Brothers.

Carney, M. (1912). *Country life and the country school.* Chicago: Row and Peterson.

Carver, F. D., and Sergiovanni, T. J. (1973). *The new school executive: a theory of administration.* New York: Mead and Dodd.

Chancellor, W. E. (1904). *Our schools: their administration and supervision.* Boston: Heath.

Chancellor, W. E. (1907). *A theory of motives, ideals, and values in education.* Boston: Houghton Mifflin.

Chancellor, W. E. (1915). *Our schools: their administration and supervision.* Rev. 1904 ed. Boston: Heath.

Charters, W. W., Jr. (1965). *Perspectives on educational administration and the behavioral sciences.* Eugene: The University of Oregon Press.

Chubb, J. E., and Moe, T. (1990). *Politics, markets and America's schools.* Washington: Brookings.

Cocking, W. D., and Williams, K. R. (1940). *The education of school administrators.* Washington, D.C.: American Council on Education.

Conley, D. T. (1993). *Roadmap to reform.* Eugene: ERIC.

Cooke, D. H. (1939). *Administering the teaching personnel.* Chicago: Benjamin H. Sanborn.

Cooper, W. J., and Koos, L. V. (eds.). (1932). *National survey of secondary education* (bulletin no. 17). Washington, D.C.: United States Office of Education.

Cooperative Study of Secondary School Standards. (1938). *How to evaluate a secondary school.* Washington, D.C.: American Council on Education.

Cox, P. W. L., and Langfitt, R. E. (1934). *High school administration and supervision.* New York: American Book Co.

Cronin, J. (1973). *The control of urban schools: perspective on the power of educational reformers.* New York: Free Press.

Cubberley, E. P. (1904). *Syllabus of lectures on the history of education, with selected bibliographies and suggestions as to reading.* New York: Macmillan.

Cubberley, E. P. (1905). *School funds and their apportionment.* New York: Teachers.

Cubberley, E. P. (1914). *State and county educational reorganization: the revised constitution and school code of the State of Osceola.* New York: Macmillan.

Cubberley, E. P. (1916). *Public school administration.* Boston: Houghton Mifflin.

Cubberley, E. P. (1923). *The principal and his school: the organization, administration and supervision of instruction in an elementary school.* Boston: Houghton Mifflin.

Cubberley, E. P. (1927). *State school administration. A textbook of principles.* Boston: Houghton Mifflin.

Cubberley, E. P. (1934). *Readings in public education in the United States.* Boston: Houghton Mifflin.

Cubberley, E. P., and Elliott, Edward. (1915). *State and county school administration.* Vol. 2. New York: Macmillan.

Culbertson, J. A. (1988). A century's quest for a knowledge base. In Boyland, N. (ed.). *Handbook on research in education.* New York: Longman, pp. 3–26.

Culp, V. H. (1942). *How to manage a rural school.* Minneapolis: Burgess Publishing Co.

Culter, H. M., and Stone, J. M. (1913). *The rural school: its methods and management.* New York: Silver Burdett.

Dewey, J., and Dewey, E. (1915). *Schools of tomorrow.* New York: E. P. Dutton.

Dewey, J. (1916). *Democracy and education.* New York: Macmillan.

Dougherty, J. H., Gorman, F. A., and Phillips, C. A. (1936). *Elementary school organization and management.* New York: Macmillan.

Dougherty, J. H. (1950). *Elementary school organization and management.* Rev. ed. New York: Macmillan.

Douglass, K. R. (1945). *Organization and administration of secondary schools.* New York: Ginn.

Dutton, S. T. (1903). *School management: practical suggestions concerning the conduct and life of the school.* New York: Scribner's.

Dutton, S. T. (1909). *School management.* Rev. 1903 ed. New York: Scribner's.

Dutton, S. T., and Snedden, D. (1908). *The administration of public education in the United States.* New York: Macmillan.

Edmondson, J. B., Roemer, J., and Bacon, F. L. (1953). *The administration of the modern secondary school.* New York: Macmillan.

Edwards, N., and Richey, H. G. (1947). *The school in the American social order.* Boston: Houghton Mifflin.

Elsbree, W., and McNally, H. J. (1951). *Elementary school administration and supervision.* New York: American Book Co.

Elsbree, W. S., and Reutter, E. E. (1954). *Staff personnel in the public schools.* New York: Prentice Hall.

Elson, R. M. (1964). *Guardians of tradition: American schoolbooks of the nineteenth century.* Lincoln: University of Nebraska Press.

English, F. W. (1992). *Educational administration: the human science.* New York: Harper-Collins.

Erickson, D. (1977). *Educational organization and administration.* Berkeley: McCutchan.

Evenden, E. S. (1933). *National survey of the education of teachers* (bulletin no. 10). Washington, D.C.: United States Office of Education.

Ford, F. A. (1958). *The Instructional program: its organization and administration.* New York: Prentice Hall.

Fox, J. H., et al. (1949). *School administration: principles and procedures.* New York: Prentice Hall.

Getzels, J., Lipham, J., and Campbell, R. F. (1968). *Educational administration as social process.* New York: Harper and Row.

Glass, T. E., Bjork, L., and Brunner, C. (2000). *The study of the American school superintendency: a look at the superintendent in the new millennium.* Arlington: American Association of School Administrators.

Goldhammer, K. (ed.). (1967). *Issues and problems in contemporary educational administration.* Eugene: Center for the Advanced Study of Educational Administration, University of Oregon.

Good, H. G., and Teller, J. D. (1969). *A history of western education.* New York: Macmillan.

Green, R. L. (2000). *Practicing the art of leadership: a problem-based approach to implementing the ISLLC standards.* Upper Saddle River: Prentice Hall.

Greider, C., and Rosenstengel, W. E. (1954). *Public school administration.* New York: Ronald.

Grieder, C., Pierce, T., and Jordan, E. F. (1961). *Public school administration.* 3rd ed. New York: Ronald.

Griffiths, D. E. (1988). Reform PDQ or RIP. Invited address. Division A, American Educational Research Association. New Orleans.

Griffiths, D. E. (ed.). (1959). *Administrative theory*. New York: Appleton-Century-Crofts.

Griffiths, D. E. (ed.). (1964). *Behavioral science and educational administration. Sixty-third yearbook of the NSSE*. Part 2. Chicago: University of Chicago Press.

Grow, H. R. (1941). *The development of guiding principles and policies for the administration of the small school system*. Lincoln: University of Nebraska.

Gulick, L., and Urwick, L. (eds.). (1937). *Papers on the science of administration*. New York: Columbia University.

Hagman, H. L. (1951). *The administration of American public schools*. New York: McGraw-Hill.

Hall, S. R. (1829). *Lectures on school-keeping*. Boston: Richardson, Lord, and Holbrook. Republished by Arno Press.

Hall, S. R. (1832). *Lectures to female teachers on school-keeping*. Boston: Richardson, Lord, and Holbrook. Republished by Arno Press.

Haller, E. J., and Strike, K. A. (1986). *An introduction to educational administration: social, legal and ethical perspectives*. New York: Longman.

Halpin, A. (ed.). (1957). *Administrative theory in education*. New York: Macmillan.

Halpin, A. (1966). *Theory and research in administration*. New York: Macmillan.

Hanson, M. (1979). *Educational administration and organizational behavior*. Boston: Allyn and Bacon.

Hanushek, E. A. (1994). *Making schools work: improving performance and controlling costs*. Washington, D.C.: Brookings.

Hanus, P. (1913). *School efficiency: a constructive study applied to New York City*. Yonkers: World Book.

Hanus, P. (1920). *School administration and school reports*. Boston: Houghton Mifflin.

Henry, N. B. (ed.). (1954). *Changing conceptions in educational administration. Forty-fifth yearbook of the NSSE*. Part 2. Chicago: University of Chicago Press.

Henry, N. B. (ed.). (1959). *Community education: principles and practices from world-wide experience. Fifty-eighth yearbook of the NSSE*. Part 1. Chicago: University of Chicago Press.

Henry, N. B. (ed.). (1953). *The community school. Fifty-second yearbook of the NSSE*. Part 2. Chicago: University of Chicago Press for the Society.

Henzlik, F. E. (1943). *School administration and education for administrative leadership in towns and villages*. Lincoln: University of Nebraska.

Hilton, E. (1949). *Rural school management.* New York: American Book Co.

Hines, L. N. (1911). The ideal school board from the superintendent's point of view. *NEA Proceedings.* Washington, D.C.: Author.

Hinsdale, R. A. (1894). The American school superintendent. *Educational Review* 7 (January): 42–54.

Hoy, W. K., and Miskel, C. G. (1978). *Educational administration: theory, research and practice.* New York: Random House.

Hoyle, J. R., English, F. W., and Steffy, B. E. (1998). *Skills for successful 21st century school leaders: standards for peak performance.* Arlington: American Association of School Administrators.

Huggett, A. J. (1950). *Practical school administration.* Champaign: Garrard Press.

Hunkins, R. V. (1931). *The superintendent at work in smaller schools.* Boston: Heath.

Immegart, G. L. (1975). *The study of educational administration 1954–74: myths, paradoxes, facts, and prospects.* Unpublished paper. Columbus: Ohio State University-UCEA.

Jaggers, R. E. (1934). *Administering the county school system.* New York: American Book Co.

Johnston, E. G. (1942). *Administering the guidance program.* Minneapolis: Educational Publishers.

Keith, S., and Girling, R. (1991). *Education, management, and participation: new directions in educational administration.* Boston: Allyn and Bacon.

Kimbrough, R. B., and Nunnery, M. Y. (1976). *Educational administration: an introduction.* New York: Macmillan.

Knezevich, S. J. (1984). *Administration of public education.* 4th ed. New York: Harper and Row.

Knight, E. W. (1953). *Readings in educational administration.* New York: Holt.

Koopman, G. R., Miel, A., and Misner, P. J. (1943). *Democracy in school administration.* New York: Appleton-Century-Crofts.

Koos, L. V. (1917). *The administration of secondary-school units.* Vol. 7. Supplementary Educational Monographs. Chicago: University of Chicago Press .

Koos, L. V., et al. (1940). *Administering the secondary school.* New York: American Book.

Kowalski, T. J., and Reitzug, U. C. (1993). *Contemporary school administration: an introduction.* White Plains: Longman.

Kowalski, T. J. (1995). *Case studies in educational Administration.* White Plains: Longman.

Langfitt, R., et al. (1936). *The small high school at work.* New York: American Book Co.

Lawson, D. E. (1953). *School administration.* New York: Odyssey Press.

Lund, J. (1942). *Education of school administrators* (bulletin 1941, no. 6, Federal Security Agency, U.S. Office of Education). Washington, D.C.: United States Government Printing Office.

Lunenburg, F. C., and Ornstein, A. C. (1996). *Educational administration: concepts and practice.* Belmont: Wadsworth.

Magill, W. H. (1941). *Administering vocational education.* Minneapolis: Educational Publishers.

McCarthy, M., and Kuh, G. (1997). *Continuity and change: the educational leadership professoriate.* Columbia: University Council on Educational Administration.

Maxwell, C. R., and Kilzer, L. R. (1936). *High school administration.* Garden City: Doubleday.

Maxwell, W. M. (1912). *A quarter century of public school development.* New York: American Book.

Melby, E. O. (1955). *Administering community education.* Englewood Cliffs: Prentice Hall.

Melchoir, W. T. (1950). *Instructional supervision: a guide to modern practice.* Boston: Heath.

Merseth, K. K. (1997). *Case studies in educational administration.* New York: Longman.

Miller, Van, Madden, G., and Kincheloe, J. R. (1968). *The public administration of American school systems.* 2nd ed. New York: Macmillan.

Moehlman, A. B. (1951). *School administration.* Boston: Houghton Mifflin.

Monahan, W. (ed.). (1975). *Theoretical dimensions of educational administration.* New York: Macmillan.

Monroe, P. (ed.). (1911). *A cyclopaedia of education.* New York: Macmillan.

Moore, H. A., Jr. (1957). *Studies in school administration: a report on the CPEA.* Washington, D.C.: AASA.

Morphet, E., Johns, R. L., and Reller, T. L. (1984). *Educational organizations and administration.* 4th ed. Englewood Cliffs: Prentice Hall.

Mort, P. R. (1946). *Principles of school administration: a synthesis of basic concepts.* New York: McGraw-Hill.

National Commission on Excellence in Education. (1983). *A nation at risk.* Washington, D.C.: USDOE.

National Education Association. (1895). *Journal of proceedings and addresses.* Washington, D.C.: Author.

National Policy Board for Educational Administration. (1989). *Improving the preparation of school administrators: an agenda for reform.* Charlottesville: Author.

Nee-Benham, M. K. P. (1999). *Case studies for school administrators.* Lancaster: Technomic.

Newell, C. (1978). *Human behavior in educational administration.* Englewood Cliffs: Prentice Hall.

Newlon, J. H. (1934). *Educational administration as social policy.* New York: Scribner's.

Newsom, N., and Langfitt, R. E. (eds.). (1940). *Administrative practices in large high schools.* New York: American Book.

Otto, H. J. (1946). *Organizational and administrative practices in elementary schools in the United States.* Austin: University of Texas.

Otto, H. J. (1954). *Elementary school organization and administration.* 3rd ed. New York: Appleton-Century-Crofts.

Ovsiew, L. (1953). *Emerging practices in school administration.* New York: Metropolitan School Study Council and Cooperative Program in Education Administration.

Owens, R. G. (1998). *Organizational behavior in education.* Boston: Allyn and Bacon.

Page, D. P. (1885). *Theory and practice of teaching* (originally published in 1847; new edition, edited and enlarged by W. H. Payne). New York: A. S. Barnes.

Payne, W. H. (1875). *Chapters on school supervision.* Cincinnati: Wilson, Hinkle, and Co.

Payne, W. H. (1901). *Education of teachers.* Richmond: B. F. Johnson.

Pennock, J. R. (1941). *Administration and the rule of law.* New York: Holt, Rinehart and Winston.

Pittinger, B. R. (1951). *Local public school administration.* New York: McGraw-Hill.

Reavis, W. C. (1938). *Critical issues in educational administration.* Chicago: University of Chicago Press.

Reavis, W. C. (1939). *Democratic practices in school administration.* Chicago: University of Chicago Press.

Reavis, W. C. (1941). *Administrative adjustments required by socio-economic change.* Chicago: University of Chicago Press.

Reavis, W. C. (1946). *Educational administration.* Chicago: University of Chicago Press.

Reavis, W. C. (1954). *Administering the elementary school—a cooperative educational enterprise.* New York: Prentice Hall.

Reeder, W. G. (1939). *The administration of pupil transportation.* Columbus: Educators Press.

Reeder, W. G. (1951). *The fundamentals of public school administration.* 3rd ed. New York: Macmillan.

Reller, T. L. (1935). *The development of the city superintendency of schools in the United States.* Philadelphia: Author.

Reller, T. L. (1941). Superintendents of schools: duties and responsibilities. In Monroe, W. S. (ed.), *Encyclopedia of educational research.* New York: Macmillan.

Sarason, S. B. (1990). *The predictable failure of educational reform.* San Francisco: Jossey-Bass.

Search, P. W. (1901). *An ideal school.* New York: Appleton.

Sears, J. B. (1925). *The school survey: a textbook on the use of school surveying in the administration of public schools.* Boston: Houghton Mifflin.

Sears, J. B. (1947). *Public school administration.* New York: Ronald.

Sears, J. B. (1950). *The nature of the administrative process.* New York: McGraw-Hill.

Sears, J. B., and Henderson, A. D. (1957). *Cubberley of Stanford.* Palo Alto: Stanford University Press.

Sergiovanni, T. J., and Carver, F. D. (1973). *The new school executive: a theory of administration.* New York: Dodd and Mead.

Shane, H. G., and Yauch, W. A. (1954). *Creative school administration in elementary and junior high schools.* New York: Holt.

Sharp, W. L., Walters, J. K., and Sharp, H. (2001). *Case studies for school leaders: implementing the ISLLC standards.* Lanham: Scarecrow.

Short, P. M., and Scribner, J. P. (2000). *Case studies of the superintendency.* Lanham: Scarecrow.

Silver, P. (1983). *Educational administration: theoretical perspectives on practice and research.* New York: Harper and Row.

Sizer, T. R. (1992). *Horace's school: redesigning the American high school.* New York: Houghton-Mifflin.

Skogsberg, A. H. (1950). *Administrative operational patterns.* New York: Metropolitan School Study, Bureau of Publications.

Spears, H. (1953). *Improving the supervision of instruction.* New York: Prentice Hall.

Strayer, G. D., and Thorndike, L. (1913). *Educational administration: quantitative studies.* New York: Macmillan.

Strayer, G. D., and Engelhardt, N. L. (1925). *Problems in educational administration.* New York: Teachers College, Columbia University.

Suzzallo, H. (1906). *The rise of local school supervision in Massachusetts.* New York: Teachers College, Columbia University.

Tiedeman, D. V. (1956). *Teacher competence and its relation to salary.* Cambridge: New England School Development Council.

Tyack, D. B., and Cuban, L. (1995). *Tinkering toward utopia: a century of public school reform.* Cambridge: Harvard University Press.

Tyack, D. B. (1976). Pilgrim's progress: toward a social history of the school superintendency, 1860–1960. *History of Education Quarterly* 16 (fall): 257–300.

Tyack, D. B., and Cummings, R. (1977). Leadership in American public schools before 1954. In Cunningham, L., Hack, W. G., and Nystrand, R. O. (eds.). *Educational administration: the developing decades.* Berkeley: McCutchan.

Tyack, D. B., and Hansot, E. (1982). *Managers of virtue: public school leadership in America, 1820–1980.* New York: Basic Books.

Tyack, D. B., Lowe, R., and Hansot, E. (1984). *Public schools in hard times.* Cambridge: Harvard University Press.

Wahlquist, J. T. (ed.). (1952). *The administration of public education.* New York: Ronald.

Weber, C. A. (1954). *Personnel problems of school administrators.* New York: McGraw-Hill.

Weber, O. F. (1930). *Problems in public school administration.* New York: Century.

Weber, S. E. (1937). *Cooperative administration and supervision of the teaching personnel.* New York: Thomas Nelson and Sons.

Wiles, K. (1950). *Supervision for better schools.* New York: Prentice Hall.

Witham, E. C. (1936). *Problem studies in school administration.* New York: Prentice Hall.

Yauch, W. A. (1949). *Improving human relations in school administration.* New York: Harper.

Yeager, W. A. (1949). *Administration and the pupil.* New York: Harper.

Yeager, W. A. (1954). *Administration and the teacher.* New York: Harper.

Index

academic freedom, 20
accrediting associations, 47
active method, 25
activities program, 58
Administering Pupil Transportation (Butterworth and Ruegsegger), 46, 57–58, 69
Administering the County School System (Jaggers), 138
Administering the Secondary School (Koos et al.), 46, 48–51, 57–58, 60, 62–64, 71, 138
Administering the Teaching Personnel (Cooke), 46–48, 50–51, 60, 62, 67
administration. *See* educational administration
The Administration of American Public Schools (Hagman), 139
The Administration of Consolidated and Village Schools (Almack and Bursch), 41, 137
Administration of Public Education (Knezevich), 91, 99–100, 140
The Administration of Public Education in the United States (Dutton and Snedden), 128, 136
The Administration of Public Education (Wahlquist), 76
The Administration of Pupil Transportation (Reeder), 139
Administrative Adjustments Required by Socio-Economic Change (Reavis), 138
Administrative Practices in Large High Schools (Newsom and Langfitt), 46, 54–55, 65, 70

administrative theory, 87, 99, 113; development of, 92–96, 139–140
Administrative Theory (Griffiths), 94
Administrative Theory in Education (ed. Halpin), 94–95, 102
administrators. *See* educational administrators
Almack, John C., 41, 137
American Association of School Administrators (AASA), 80, 83
American Educational Research Association, 7, 112
American educational system, 3, 4, 66
American Historical Association, 66
Americanism, 4, 75
American School Finance Association, 7
aristocratic education, 23–24
Ashbaugh, Carl, 116, 122, 141
average practice, 69–70, 132
Ayer, Fred C., 137

back-to-the-liberal-arts movement, 25
Bagley, William Chandler, 41
Barnes, Ina G., 40, 41, 137
Barr, A. S., 137
behavioral and social sciences, 5, 87, 88–89, 101–103, 134
belief system, 103
Berliner, David, 111
best practices compendiums, 8, 18, 27, 92, 133, 136
Bible, 2
Biddle, Bruce, 111
Blue Law contracts, 50–51
bottom-up reforms, 109–110
Brown, Edwin J., 138

Brown v. Board of Education, 77
Bursch, James, 41, 137
business interests, 23–24
business managers, 14–15, 128
Butterworth, Julian E., 40–41, 46, 57–58, 69

Callahan, Raymond, 40
Campbell, Roald, 91, 95, 100–102, 134, 140
capitalist oppression, 27–28
Carney, Mabel, 40, 137
Carver, Fred D., 91, 102–104, 140
Case Studies for School Administrators (Nee-Benham), 117, 123, 141
Case Studies for School Leaders: Implementing the ISLLC Standards (Sharp, Walters, and Sharp), 117, 123, 141
Case Studies for the Superintendency (Short and Scribner), 117, 123, 141
Case Studies in Educational Administration (Kowalski), 122, 141
Case Studies in Educational Administration (Merseth), 117, 122, 141
case studies textbooks, 8, 107, 114–117, 121–123, 140–141
Castetter, William, 107
"A Century's Quest for a Knowledge Base" (Culbertson), 113
certification, 47–49, 62
Chancellor, William E., 16–17, 22–24, 28, 32–34, 128, 136–137
change models, 106
Changing Conceptions of Education (Cubberley), 35, 130
Chapters on School Supervision (Payne), 16, 17, 19–20, 136
child-centered school, 18, 25, 128
citizenship, 24, 25
City School Administration course (Cubberley), 39
city schools, 13–14, 24, 110, 128
Cleveland Plan, 15
Cocking, Walter D., 70, 138
Commissioner of Education, 36, 41
Committee for the Advancement of School Administration, 83
Committee of Fifteen, 15
Committee on the Orientation of Second-

ary Education, Department of Secondary School Principals (NEA), 55–56, 58
common school movement, 2, 127, 128–129
commonsense principles, 17, 98, 138
community relations, 20–22, 107, 133
community schools, 75, 77–81
Conference of Administrative Officers of Public and Private Schools, 58
Conley, David, 111
connectionist theory, 4
consultative services, 59–60
Contemporary School Administration: An Introduction (Kowalski and Reitzug), 116, 120–121, 141
Continuity and Change: The Educational Leadership Professoriate (McCarthy and Kuh), 112
cookbook approach, 4–5, 8, 83, 92, 111, 136
Cooke, Dennis H., 45–48, 50–51, 60, 62, 67
Cooper, William J., 70
Cooperative Administration and Supervision of the Teaching Personnel (Weber), 46–50, 59, 62, 67, 138
Cooperative Program in Educational Administration, 83
Cornell University, 41
Country Life and the Country School (Carney), 40, 137
Cox, Phillip L., 46, 56–58, 63, 65, 71
critical theory, 9–10
Cronin, J., 28
Cuban, Larry, 111
Cubberley, Ellwood Patterson, 16, 18, 26–27, 34–42, 56–57, 78, 98, 130
Culbertson, Jack, 113
Culp, Vernon H., 46, 52–54, 58
Culter, Horace M., 137
curriculum, 58–59
Cyclopaedia of Education (Monroe), 31, 35, 129, 137

democracy, 77–79
Democracy and Education (Dewey), 24
"Democracy for the Teacher" (Dewey), 68
Democracy in School Administration

(Koopman, Miel, and Misner), 46, 59–60, 67–68, 70–71, 133, 138
democratic administration, 67–69, 75, 77–81, 132, 138
Democratic Practices in School Administration (Reavis), 138
democratic principles, 53, 66, 79
Department of Superintendence (NEA), 13, 15
descriptive texts, 97–100
Dewey, Evelyn, 17–18
Dewey, John, 4, 17–18, 25, 68, 128, 133
direct method, 26
disciplinary problems, 21
Division A (administration), 7, 112
doctoral dissertations, 5, 34, 95, 115
Dougherty, James H., 46, 52, 53, 67
Douglass, K. R., 57, 61–62, 68–69, 71
dualism, 45, 69–70, 131
dual-leadership system, 14–15, 128
Dutton, Samuel Train, 16–18, 21, 24, 26, 32–34, 36, 127, 128, 136

Education, Management, and Participation: New Directions in Educational Administration (Keith and Girling), 116, 119–120, 141
education, purposes of, 66–67, 70, 131, 132
educational administration, 31–32; democratic, 67–69, 75, 77–81, 138; differentiation of, 56; functions of, 70–72; in higher-education institutions, 129–130; literature of, 1–2; purposes of, 132–133; scientific basis for, 81–82; shift toward academics, 14–17; societal reform and, 65; standardization movement, 8–9, 109, 124–125, 134
Educational Administration: An Introduction (Kimbrough and Nunnery), 91, 104–105, 140
Educational Administration: Concepts and Practices (Lunenburg and Ornstein), 116–118, 124, 141
Educational Administration: Quantitative Studies (Strayer and Thorndike), 34–35, 137
"Educational Administration: Reform PDQ or RIP" (Griffiths), 112–113

Educational Administration: The Human Science (English), 116, 118–119, 141
Educational Administration: Theory, Research, and Practice (Hoy, Miskel, and Forsyth), 91, 105, 116–117, 124, 141
Educational Administration and Organization: Concepts, Practices, and Issues (Morphet, Johns, and Reller), 91, 98–99, 140
Educational Administration and Organizational Behavior (Hanson), 92, 106, 140
Educational Administration As a Social Process (Getzels, Lipham, and Campbell), 91, 101–102, 104, 134, 140
Educational Administration As Social Policy (Newlon), 46, 66, 70, 71–72, 132, 138
educational administrators: academic and professional qualifications, 61–62; certification of, 62; duties of, 62–63; professional organizations, 6–7; profession of preparing, 3–4; reform of programs, 112–113; salaries, 64–65; as social scientists, 6. *See also* principals; superintendents
Educational Leadership: Case Studies for Reflective Practice (Ashbaugh and Kasten), 116, 122, 141
educational parks, 18, 25
The Educational Review (NEA), 36
Educational Testing Service, 8
Education and Public Understanding (McCloskey), 107
Education and the Cult of Efficiency (Cubberley), 16, 18, 26–27, 34, 36
Education Department, 110
Education of School Administrators (Lund), 70
The Education of School Administrators (Cocking and Williams), 70, 138
Education of Teachers (Payne), 16, 136
Edwards, Newton, 138
efficiency, 23–24, 40, 69, 79
elected school director, 15
Elementary School Administration and Supervision (Elsbree and McNally), 139
Elementary School Organization and Management (Dougherty, Gorman, and Phillips), 46, 52, 53, 67

elementary schools, 50, 52–54
Elliott, Edward, 36
Elsbree, Willard, 139
empiricism, 34–35, 136
Engelhardt, N. L., 42, 137
English, Fenwick W., 116, 118–119, 121–122, 141
Evenden, Edward S., 70
evolution, 26
expert opinion, 97, 98, 104, 133, 136
extracurriculum, 58

factualism, 88, 134
Follett, Mary Parker, 4
Ford, Frederick A., 46
Forsyth, Patrick, 105, 116
Fox, James H., 139
function analysis, 97
The Fundamentals of Public School Administration (Reeder), 41

gardens, student, 25–26
general-type texts, 89–90, 95, 105–106, 114–115, 120–121
George Peabody College, 16, 94
Getzels, Jacob, 91, 101–102, 104, 134, 140
Girling, Robert, 116, 119–120, 141
Gorman, Frank A., 46, 52, 53, 67
Great Depression, 45, 49–50, 65, 131, 138
Green, Reginald, 116, 123, 141
Grieder, Calvin, 91
Griffiths, Daniel, 6, 94, 112–113
Guba, Egon, 101
Gulick, Luther, 4

Hagman, Harlan, 139
Hall, G. Stanley, 17, 25
Hall, Samuel R., 16–17, 19–21, 136
Haller, Emil, 116, 121, 141
Halpin, Andrew, 94–95, 102
Handbook on Research in Educational Administration, 113
Hanson, Mark, 92, 106–107, 140
Hansot, Elisabeth, 127
Hanus, Paul, 137
Harland, Sidney, 18
Harris, William Torrey, 25
High School Administration and Supervision (Cox and Langfitt), 46, 56–58, 63, 65, 71

home visits, 21
Horace's School (Sizer), 111
hot topic books, 10
Houghton Mifflin, 35, 41
How to Evaluate a Secondary School (Cooperative Study of Secondary School Standards), 70
How to Manage a Rural School (Culp), 46, 52–54, 58
Hoy, Wayne, 91, 105, 116–117, 124, 141
Hoyle, John, 116, 121–122, 141
Human Behavior in Educational Administration (Newell), 91, 105–106, 140
humanists, 138
human relations theory, 4
Hunkins, R. V., 41

An Ideal School (Search), 16, 17–18, 24–26, 136
Improving Education of School Administrators: An Agenda for Reform, 112
Improving Human Relations in School Administration (Yauch), 76, 139
individual differences of students, 25
The Instructional Program: Its Organization and Administration (Ford), 46, 59
Interstate School Leader Licensing Consortium (ISLLC), 8
Investigation of the Social Studies in the Schools (AHA), 66
ISLLC standards, 123, 124

Jaggers, Richard E., 138
job analysis model, 40
Johns, Roe, 91, 98–99, 140
Jordan, E. Forbis, 91
Journal of Proceedings and Addresses (NEA), 36, 136
junior college, 54

Kasten, Katherine L., 116, 122, 141
Kefauver, 77–78
Keith, Sherry, 116, 119–120, 141
Kellogg Foundation, 94
Kenezevich, Steven, 91
Kimbrough, Ralph, 91, 104–105, 140
Kincheloe, James B., 96, 140
Kincheloe, Joseph, 91
Knezevich, Steven, 91, 99–100, 140
Knight, Edgar W., 77, 78

Koopman, Robert G., 45, 46, 59–60, 67–68, 70–71, 133, 138
Koos, Leonard V., 46, 48–51, 57–58, 60, 62–64, 70–71, 138
Kowalski, Theodore, 116, 120–122, 141
Kuh, George, 112

Langfitt, R. Emerson, 46, 54–58, 63, 65, 70, 71
Lawson, Douglas E., 77, 81
lay communities, 21
leadership, 100, 120–121; dual system, 14–15, 128
Lectures on School-Keeping (Hall), 16, 19–21, 136
Lectures to Female School Teachers on School-Keeping (Hall), 16, 20, 136
licensing requirements, 8
Lipham, James, 91, 101–102, 104, 134, 140
Local Public School Administration (Pittinger), 76, 139
Lund, John, 70
Lunenburg, Fred C., 116–118, 124, 141

Macmillan Company, 34, 35, 40–41
Madden, George, 91, 96, 140
male chauvinism, 20, 33
management science, 103
Managers of Virtue: Public School Leadership in America, 1920–1980 (Tyack and Hansot), 127, 131
Mann, Horace, 127
The Manufactured Crisis (Berliner and Biddle), 111
Maxwell, William H., 37, 137
McCarthy, Martha, 112
McCarthyism, 139
McCloskey, Gordon, 107
McGuffey's Readers, 2
McNally, Harold, 139
Merseth, Katherine, 117, 141
Midwest Administration Center, 94, 95, 102
Miel, Alice, 45, 46, 59–60, 67–68, 70–71, 133, 138
Miller, Van, 91, 96–98, 140
Miskel, Cecil, 91, 105, 116–117, 124, 141

Misner, Paul, 45, 46, 59–60, 67–68, 70–71, 133, 138
Moehlman, Arthur B., 76, 139
Monahan, William, 91, 140
Monroe, Paul, 31, 35, 129, 137
Moore, Hollis, 82
moral values, 3–4, 17–18, 21–22, 103, 127–128
Morphet, Edgar, 91, 98–99, 140
Mort, Paul R., 76, 78, 82–83, 92–93, 133, 139
multiple editions, 92, 115, 124, 135

National Commission on Excellence in Education, 109
National Conference of Professors of Educational Administration (NCPEA), 7, 80, 83
National Education Association (NEA), 6–7, 36, 55–56, 58, 130, 136; Department of Superintendence, 13, 15
National Policy Board for Educational Administration, 8, 112
National Survey of the Education of Teachers, 46–47, 51
A Nation at Risk, 109, 134
The Nature of the Administrative Process (Sears), 76, 92–93, 139
Nee-Benham, M. K., 117, 123, 141
neoconservative politics, 110–111
New Education, 18
Newell, Clarence, 91, 105–106, 140
Newlon, Jesse H., 45–46, 66–67, 70, 132, 138
The New School Executive (Sergiovanni and Carver), 91, 102–104, 140
Newsom, William N., 46, 54–55, 65, 70
normal schools, 3, 47
Nunnery, Michael, 91, 104–105, 140

one-room school, 53
order, 19–22
organization, democratic principles of, 79
Organizational Behavior in Education (Owens), 117, 120, 141
organizational theory, 101–102, 134
The Organization and Control of American Schools (Campbell et al.), 91, 100–101, 140

The Organization of Supervision (Ayer and Barr), 137
Ornstein, Allan, 116–118, 124, 141
Our Schools: Their Administration and Supervision (Chancellor), 16–17, 32–34, 136–137
Owens, Robert, 117, 120, 141

Page, David A., 16–21, 136
Papers on the Science of Administration (Gulick and Urwick), 78
parents, 21
Payne, William H., 16, 17, 19–20, 127, 136
perfection, 28
personnel administration, 107
Phillips, Claude A., 46, 52, 53, 67
physical health, 25
Pierce, Thomas, 91
Pittinger, Benjamin R., 76, 79, 139
policy-directed texts, 100–101, 111
political opportunism, 110–111
postmodernism, 9–10
practice-oriented textbooks, 18, 109
practice-theory dualism, 69–70, 88–90, 124
Practicing the Art of Leadership: A Problem-Based Approach to Implementing the ISLLC Standards (Green), 116, 123, 141
The Predictable Failure of Educational Reform (Sarason), 111
The Principal and His School (Cubberley), 36, 39, 40
principals, 9, 19; roles, 60–61; of secondary schools, 54–55; selection of teachers and, 62–63; training of, 3–4
principles, 93
Principles of Rural School Administration (Butterworth), 40–41
Principles of School Administration: A Synthesis of Basic Concepts (Mort), 76, 82–83, 93, 139
private sector, 10
Problems in Educational Administration (Strayer and Engelhardt), 42, 137
Problems in Public School Administration (Weber), 42, 137
Problem Studies in School Administration (Witham), 138
process conceptualization, 83

professional legitimacy, 6
professional organizations, 6–7, 31
professors: aging of, 11; publication of textbooks, 3–5, 32; reform proposals and, 112; selection of student texts, 113–114; specialization, 6–7; as sponsors of superintendents, 130–131; vs. practitioners, 6–7, 135
progressive education movement, 4, 17, 58
Protestant views, 135, 136
The Public Administration of American School Systems (Miller), 91, 96–98, 140
public relations, 20–21
Public School Administration (Cubberley), 35, 36–39, 56, 137
Public School Administration (Grieder, Pierce, and Jordan), 91, 98
publishers, 10, 113–114, 124–125, 134

qualitative research, 115
quantitative works, 34–35
A Quarter Century of Public Development (Maxwell), 37, 137

rationality, 21
reading instruction, 26
Readings in Educational Administration (Knight), 77
Reagan Administration, 110
Reavis, William C., 138
Rebore, Ronald, 107
Reeder, Ward, 41, 139
reform, 109–111, 134, 140–141; of preparation programs, 112–113
reform literature, 109, 132, 134–135
regional teachers colleges, 32
Reitzug, Ulrich, 116, 120–121, 141
religion, 127–129
Reller, Theodore, 91, 98–99, 140
research, 105, 115
revisionist arguments, 27–28
Richey, Herman, 138
Riverside Series, 35–36, 41
Roadmap to Reform (Conley), 111
Ruegsegger, Virgil, 46, 57–58, 69
rural education, 40–41
Rural Education Series (Macmillan), 40–41

Rural Life and Education (Cubberley), 41

Rural School Management (Barnes), 40, 137

Rural School Management (Culp), 52

rural schools, 52–54, 58

The Rural School: Its Methods and Management (Culter and Stone), 137

salaries: administrators, 64–65; teachers, 49–52, 64

Sarason, Seymour, 111

scholarly books, 111

School Administration: Principles and Procedures(Fox), 139

School Administration and School Reports (Hanus), 137

School Administration (Lawson), 77

School Administration (Moehlman), 76, 139

school administration *vs.* educational administration, 79–80

school boards, 4, 26, 34, 127; order and, 19; rating system, 60; selection of teachers and, 62–63; size and compensation, 34, 39; small and rural schools, 53; ward boards, 13–14, 28, 49–50; women on, 33

school districts, 13–14, 110

School Efficiency: A Constructive Study Applied to New York City (Hanus), 137

school executive, as term, 102, 103

school finance, 22, 26, 42

The School in the American Social Order (Edwards and Richey), 138

school law, 38, 42, 107, 118, 119

School Management: Practical Suggestions Concerning the Conduct and Life of the School (Dutton), 16, 21, 26, 32–34, 136

School Public Administration (Sears), 76, 139

schools, roles of, 45, 87–88, 95

Schools of Tomorrow (Dewey and Dewey), 17–18

school surveys, 26, 37–38, 46–47, 69–70, 131, 136

The School Survey: A Textbook on the Use of School Surveying in the Administration of Public Schools (Sears), 137

science-of-education movement, 18–19, 25–27, 69

scientific management, 3–4, 6, 130, 131, 136

scientific method, 66

Scribner, Jay P., 117, 123, 141

Search, Preston V., 16, 17–18, 24–26, 136

Sears, Jesse B., 76, 79–81, 83, 92–93, 133, 137

secondary education, growth of, 54–56

Secondary School Administration (Brown), 138

secondary schools, 4, 47, 50, 53

senior high school, 50, 51

Sergiovanni, Thomas, 91, 102–104, 140

Sharp, Helen, 117, 123, 141

Sharp, William, 117, 123, 141

Short, Paula, 117, 123, 141

Sizer, Theodore, 111

Skills for Successful 21st Century School Leaders: Standards for Peak Performers (Hoyle, English, and Steffy), 116, 121–122, 141

Snedden, David A., 16–18, 26–27, 34, 36, 128

social analysis, 41. *See also* behavioral and social sciences

socialization, 53, 56, 58, 66–67

social movements, 113

social statesmanship, 77–78

societal emphases, 77

societal reform, 65

sovereignty, 19–20

Spalding, Willard, 96

special-interest groups, 7

specialization, 107, 136

specialized textbooks, 6–7, 75–76, 90, 104, 107, 114, 131

standards, 8–9, 109, 124–125, 134

Stanford University, 35

State and County, School Administration (Cubberley and Elliott), 36

State and County Educational Reorganization (Cubberley), 38

State and County School Administration (Cubberley), 38

State School Administration: A Textbook of Principles (Cubberley), 42, 137

statistics, 100, 130

Steffy, Betty, 116, 121–122, 141
Stone, Julia M., 137
Strayer, George D., 18, 34, 42, 57, 130, 137
Strike, Kenneth, 116, 121, 141
The Superintendent at Work in Smaller Schools (Hunkins), 41
superintendents, 9, 19, 48, 62, 102, 128; 1800s, 13–16; professors as sponsors for, 130–131; qualities, 39–40; roles, 60–61
supervision, 59–60, 75–76
Survey of Rural Education, 41
surveys. *See* school surveys

Taylor, Frederick, 3, 130
teacher colleges, 5
teacher evaluations, 20, 59
teacher preparation, 46–47
teachers: appointment, 14–15; certification, 48–49; democratic administration and, 67–69; moral dedication of, 21; salaries and work loads, 49–52, 64; sovereignty, 20; subject areas, 51; women, 50–51
Teachers College, 21, 32, 34–35, 39
Teachers College Contributions to Education Series, 35
teacher supply, 47, 49
teacher-training institutions, 47–48
technology, 87–88
test scores, 109, 110, 134
textbook eras: 1820–1914, 13–29, 128–130, 135–136; 1829–1908, 16–17; 1915–1933, 31–44, 136–137; 1934–1945, 45–73, 130–132, 138; 1946–1955, 75–86, 133–134, 138–139; 1955–1985, 87–108, 139–140; 1985–2000, 109–126, 140–141; overview, 1820–2000, 127–135
textbooks: administration, curriculum making, and supervision, 56–60; case studies, 8, 107, 114–117, 121–123, 140–141; cookbook approach, 4–5, 8, 83, 92, 111, 136; costs, 10, 114; factualism to theory in, 88–90; format, 82; general-type texts, 89–90, 95, 105–106, 114–115, 120–121; literature lists, 57; practice-oriented, 82–83; practice-theory dualism, 69–70; on principalship, 9;

professional organizations and, 6–7; publishers, 10, 113–114, 124–125, 134; specialized, 6–7, 75–76, 90, 104, 107, 114, 131; standardization movement and, 8–9, 109, 124–125, 134; theory-based, 91, 101–107; trends in, 96–101
theological allusions, 22
Theoretical Dimensions of Educational Administration (Monahan), 91, 104, 140
Theory and Practice of Teaching (Page), 16–17, 19–21, 136
Theory and Research in Administration (Halpin), 95
theory-based texts, 91, 101–107
theory movement, 5–6, 112, 113
A Theory of Motives, Ideals, and Values in Education (Chancellor), 16, 22–24, 136
Thorndike, Edward L., 18, 34–35, 137
Thorndike, Robert, 130
Tinkering toward Utopia: A Century of Public School Reform (Tyack and Cuban), 111
top-down reforms, 109, 134
totalitarianism, 77
trade books, 10
traditionalists, 71, 97–98, 104–105
transportation, 18, 53, 57–58
Tyack, David, 28, 111, 127

United Nations, 75
universities, 3
University Council on Educational Administration, 7, 83, 94, 95, 112, 135
University of Chicago, 94, 102

vertical integration, 51, 53
vocational training, 55, 58

Wahlquist, John T., 76, 79
Walters, John, 117, 123, 141
ward boards, 13–14, 28, 49–50
Weber, Oscar, 42, 137
Weber, Samuel E., 46–50, 47, 59, 62, 67, 138
Williams, Kenneth R., 70, 138
Witham, Ernest C., 138
World War II, 75, 133

Yauch, Wilbur A., 76, 79, 139